Among
The Dead

My Years in The Port Mortuary

JOHN W. HARPER

ISBN: 1530388465
ISBN 13: 9781530388462
Library of Congress Control Number: 2016905811
CreateSpace Independent Publishing Platform
North Charleston, South Carolina

For My Dear Mortuary & Military Friends

Some other day time will carry this old friend home,
Back to that place in this lonely world that touched my soul,
Recalling your friendship guarantees that I'm never alone,
Kindness and compassion you've shared makes my heart smile,

It's true that time and space separates us, but I have never been
gone,
The truth of the matter is that not a one of us could ever be
separated,
We breathe the same air and seek the same happiness and
truths,
Into this wonderful, incredulous, spectacular world we came as
one,
Bound by outside forces, that may not be seen, but can never be
undone,

Those warm souls sent to teach us may be sought, but can't be
found,
You each are a part of my family though we don't share the
same blood,
A friend that changed my world, my life, forever for the better,

Doing it simply, without a care in the world, and being your
true self,
Seldom in this existence are we blessed with such a profound
gift,

Today and every day you awake with your future at your feet,
This friend; locked into your soul, sends unconditional love,
On this day and the next, you can accomplish anything you
choose,
Choose wisely my dear friend, for time on this earth is a gift
from above,

The path that you are on is not easy; it isn't supposed to be,
Lessons abound though, so open your eyes and be aware of your
world,
Accept responsibility, step up and believe in how powerful you
are,
Faith will guide your destiny, and your will can never be denied,

The answer to any and all questions is determination, faith and
love,
So from me your brother, if you feel anything that I have said,
Know that I believe in what I say, I believe in you, and I believe
in love,
We will forever be together, whether here or above.

Special thanks must first go out to my dear friends, fellow military service members and teammates on The Dover DERT Team. Each has been unconditionally supportive of my work during the preparation of this manuscript. Though they have their own busy lives, they were generous in taking time out of those lives to assist me in recalling the details of this story. This book is a much more accurate presentation of those years, because of the team's input.

Also, I am so thankful to have a loving and caring family. My wife Mary (daughter of a Marine, mother of a Soldier, and the wife of an Airman), my son Jeremy (Army Veteran), my sister Brenda, and my parents have been the foundation of my life and have made all hopes and dreams possible. Not for one second of this existence have I ever doubted my family's undying love for me. My wife and son went above and beyond in volunteering to help with all editing, and writing chores. I did not always take their professional advice, but this never stopped them from trying to improve the grammar and flow of this manuscript.

Finally, I must thank my fellow DERT Team member Daniel Hines who willingly shared with me the challenge coin that he created honoring our team. This is the same one adorning the cover of this book.

TABLE OF CONTENTS

INTRODUCTION

Today in America we live in a politically divisive, media-driven society. There are those individuals seeking conflict, determined to create more controversy. Therefore, there may be some that do not receive the message of service and love in this manuscript, or may even portray it in an untoward light. The team and this writer understand this, but we feel that this is a story that must be shared. We believe it will touch many hearts; possibly could help a few in their recoveries from trauma, and may allow others better insight, understanding and appreciation of military service. The topics included in this book would certainly have the capability of being seen as controversial, as it touches on often considered taboo subjects. What I want to assure the reader from the beginning is that this is not meant in that way. Rather this is a personal account, with memories shared from my interviews with other team members that were on-station with me during these years. Our remembrances may not have always been exact, so we always erred on the side of caution. Even more importantly, our memories have been shared out of love for our fellow team members, and those fallen American heroes whom we served with dignity, honor, and respect.

There has been a multitude of stories written about the Dover Port Mortuary. When I search for information on the internet I find many articles written by newspaper and magazine authors, a book written and published based on the authors visit and interviews at Dover, and some professionally produced videos. The difference that you will find in this manuscript is that throughout the process of facing this tragedy post 9/11 this author and those with whom I speak about were immediately serving in the mortuary building. We share this first-hand perspective to allow the reader some opportunity to feel the tremendous love that our team felt for those fallen heroes that we served. The time that we spent in that building as a team now defines our lives. If you were to ask anyone of those team members about their time in the military, their first response and most vivid remembrances will always return to that small military base along America's most eastern shore.

This book does not represent official views of the United States Air Force, Dover Air Force Base, Office of The Armed Forces Medical Examiner or the Dover Port Mortuary. There are no shared secrets in this manuscript, and *any factual data I provide* could easily be googled and found in minutes on the internet. These views are mine and the team's alone. We are very proud of our service and want to share our feelings and personal stories with others who may find inspiration and hope in the pages to follow. Many years ago it started as notes to myself, and only took on this form after a long and reflective consideration of what I was trying to achieve. I hope to achieve two primary objectives. First, I wanted the service documented for our team and our families. I want our grandchildren to know about the sacred role we played following 9/11. Second, I wanted to assure the team that there is always hope. That if you keep working, and you never give up, ultimately you will be able to recover and move forward from the pain of the trauma that we each suffered individually in varying degrees at the port mortuary during those years.

There is plenty of self-disclosure in this book, and it is written for a reason. Though I have never been personally diagnosed with post-traumatic stress disorder, I certainly have experienced a multitude of the symptoms. However, I am in first-hand contact with some of those who were diagnosed, and I will always respect and support their struggle with their pain, and honor their privacy. My personal experience with recovery from the trauma is that the symptoms have gradually lessened over the years since I worked in the mortuary. My demeanor is much calmer, and I feel very hopeful for the future. I continue to look forward with my goals and dreams. While I do continue to suffer occasional recall and dreams from the mortuary, they are much less intense, and I remember few of the details.

Regardless of my experience, I want to be clear that I understand that my recovery may be very different from yours. I am not certain that there is one correct manner to recover. I hope that if you are suffering you will realize that there is hope for the future. I pray that you will not harm yourself, and that you will immediately seek medical attention. There is help available, but it very well may be you who has to take that first step. Tell a friend or family member if you are able. Personal trauma is incredibly difficult to disclose. No one wants to be thought of as weak. And for veterans this is especially a problem. You have been taught to be tough, to be invincible, and to fight to the end. I understand exactly where you are coming from, but please remember sometimes we all need help. If you are a veteran there is always a contact for you. The Veterans Crisis Line is a 24/7 national helpline, and you can reach them at 1-800-273-8255.

This book represents only a tiny portion of the overall Dover Port Mortuary detail, and only a small portion of time. My coverage in this manuscript extends from 9/11 until the spring of 2006. Many came before our team and many came after, and many continue to serve today. The dental piece of the mission was also small, but we treated it as the most important job in the world. All of these years later the team unanimously agrees that this was the greatest duty of our lives. Our team reported to the Armed Forces Medical Examiner, though we were working inside the mortuary building. I liken us to a single anonymous cog on a wheel. We were not a significant, politically prominent, or flashy piece of the process, but we played a critical role just the same. Day in, and day out for those years that I was on station, our team served with determination, stamina, and the will to successfully complete our specific mission. That was the mission of the *most sacred military obligation* of returning those fallen American heroes home.

There is the possibility that some of the graphic detail presented may alarm some. Let me assure you that the horrendous brutalities of our duties were tempered in this manuscript. I do not try to alarm, shock, or overwhelm your senses. Violence is a piece of the war that is real. There is no describing it in a soft way, and sugar-coating it would only be disrespecting the service of our fallen heroes. After much thought I have decided to include some of the visions as accurately as I was able, as I believe it to be much more respectful to those fallen heroes, and to our humanity itself. We live in a violent society, and unfortunately that violence is often glamourized. You can see it in television, movies or music. The vast majority of Americans hardly bat an eye. Let me share my first-hand knowledge with you that when young men and women die in war, it is not pretty, and it is not glamourous. Indeed, it is often horrific beyond description. We should never forget the horrors of war. Maybe by pointing this out it will make you think a little bit longer about that entertainment which you allow into your world.

As you read through these memories, always keep in mind that this is the story of our team's service to fallen American heroes. While the team faced their own struggles, we never lost sight of our primary mission of serving those who had sacrificed their lives for our democracy, and our freedom. *Those fallen American warriors are the true heroes of this story.* It is because of this fact, that a portion of the proceeds from this book will be donated to the Dover Fisher House for Families of the Fallen. It was opened in a ribbon-cutting ceremony on November 10th, 2010 on Dover Air Force Base. This home provides a refuge for the fallen heroes' family-members traveling to Dover. It was created to provide comfort and solace for those families dealing with the loss of their loved ones, and the worst of war. The short-term lodging provided by the Dover Fisher House is available at no cost to the families, and operates strictly through donations.

Fisher Houses have supported military families and veterans for over two decades. Though the Dover Fisher Home was the fiftieth one constructed, it was unlike the others. Rather than being located adjacent to a military hospital or Veteran's

Administration medical center, it is adjacent to the Center for Families of the Fallen, where those families attending the dignified transfer services are able to receive comfort and support. The center also provides a contact point, allowing families to gain assistance with follow-up services as they grieve the loss of their loved one.

While the account is centered on the Dover Air Force Base, the story is about much more than just our specific service inside the walls of the port mortuary. This is a story of hope and recovery. Working with human remains took an incredible emotional toll on our team. Many of us suffered the symptoms of post-traumatic stress disorder, and struggled with those feelings for many years after our mortuary service ended. This book will take the reader inside of that service, and share some of those duties that contributed to these feelings. Like all great struggles in our lives, time usually will sort out our feelings, and ultimately make us feel better. Today the majority has recovered in varying degrees and leads productive and meaningful lives. I am very proud to have been a part of this team, and this story is dedicated to them.

John W. Harper
Orlando, Florida, USA

1

DEATH IN AMERICA

My relationship with death has changed over the years. I've experienced it personally with family and friends, and through my military service I have looked it directly in the eye. I respect death, just as I respect life. Due to my service in the mortuary, I have spent much time in reflection over the years, and have made peace with death. This acceptance has helped to fill my life with hope and joy. My prayer is that you will not avoid the topic. Rather I wish for you to embrace the reality that you will also pass through the doors of this world. Live and enjoy your moments and years, for soon it will be your time to depart.

This concept of death is a topic that is mostly avoided by the majority of Americans. There are many reasons for this, foremost of which is the fact that we live in a youth-worshipping society, where the media concentrates the lens of life on those who are young and beautiful. Our lives and minds are shaped by the incessant beat of the media's drums. We buy in, we believe, and seldom take the time in our busy lives to consider what an incredibly important part of our existence depends upon death. Additionally, death tends to be one of those subjects seldom brought up in conversation. It is only addressed head-on when it becomes a necessity to accommodate our lives, or that of our families or friends. This is not a bad thing, I would just ask you to consider the subject a bit more broadly.

Death provides a limit to our existence, and when embraced can provide a framework for our lives. As we become aware and accept that we will also pass, these insights provides us the encouragement to progress with our lives, set goals and achieve our dreams. Each of us is on a clock and our time on this planet is limited, though we never know when that chime is going to strike midnight. If we begin to see death as our companion, and a passage through this world then we suddenly begin to feel a greater continuity with the flow of life. Maybe we can even learn to live our lives, rather than just passing through.

There has always been the old adage and associated thought that the number of years lived are a less important gauge of the quality of our lives, than the life that we have put into those years. So it is that some people, who have lived only twenty-five years, may have enjoyed a fuller life than another who lives until age eighty. By fully living, I do not maintain that you must race through your existence. Rather, I suggest truly living each day as it is the last one that you will ever have. One day that will be the case, and probably much sooner than any of us believe.

If you haven't already done so in your life, try to determine what you love most, and to follow that path. Start small and grow. If you love flowers, than plant one and watch it grow. Allow yourself to be amazed by the fascinating circle of life that all living earthly things must dance along. If you want to become a black belt in karate, then start today. You must know that all black belts were once novice white belts with a dream, and fully determined to learn the required skills. If this is your path, jump on it fast and hard. No matter your age, just get out there and go for it. You are a human being. You are an incredible creation, full of power beyond your greatest imagination. You can do anything that you choose to do.

Be good to yourself, and put yourself first. Honor your time, and respect the importance of each moment. Examine your own thoughts and feelings, wishes and dreams. Are you happy with who you are, and where you are? If so, good for you, keep moving along the path. If not, change course immediately. Take one small step, pick up the pace, and then run. Do not let your dreams be interfered with. Do not worry that no one believes you, or believes in you. Believe in yourself, and the world will open a path to your every dream.

All individuals have personal beliefs about the after-life. And it should be mentioned that some believe in no after-life at all. Regardless of what you believe, you are by default an extension of those beliefs. Do not let those beliefs constrain your possibility of thought. Do not allow those thoughts to contain you in a box. Be open to possibility. You are not as brilliant or wise as you think you are, and neither am I. We all have much to learn if only we are receptive and remain open to those around us. Talk a little less, listen a little more. Find someone who believes something different from you, and find out why they are so sure of that belief. How do they know what is going to happen? Why do they believe this? Surround yourself with, and stay open to those who are willing to share, and willing to help you continue to grow.

This book will be an examination and reflection of the chaos that an untimely and violent death creates. Further, this chaos is capable of creating great pain for all those surrounding that immediate death. As you read through these pages, do not allow yourself to think of these fallen heroes apart from yourself. They were someone's father or mother, brother, sister or child. You are them. I am them. The thread of life ties each of us together, whether or not we are willing to consider it. You can amuse yourself with the idea that we are all different in a thousand ways, but in reality we are alike in a million ways. We are all intimately connected, and life on this planet exists as one.

Of the thousands of human remains that I personally and intimately worked with over those years in the mortuary, very few of those souls expected to be lying cold and still on that frigid table in the port mortuary. As I stare down at them, some lay there solemnly seeming content with the world that they had departed, while many others shared a face full of fright. The death mask is telling. Those deceased heroes had awoken the morning of their deaths with no inkling at all that this would be their final day in this world. But, it was. The majority of these souls had very little control over the events or war, and the ultimate demise that they suffered.

Our lives or at least the majority of our lives and deaths will be different. Many of us will know as we approach that door of passage. It is called old age, if we're fortunate enough to enjoy it. This is a great gift to each of us as we measure the lives that we have lived. Today you awoke to another day on this small mote of dust, catapulting through space, and spinning unnoticed amid an immeasurable universe. Today life on this planet is a miracle, and you are a miracle. Make the most of it. No matter if you fail or succeed today, just be sure that you learn and grow from that experience. We are all in a state of constant flux, and this is a very good thing. I am thankful to be on this journey through space and time with you. Let's continue to grow together.

2

MILITARY SERVICE

Military service is a very individual pursuit. In this nation, we no longer draft our young men or women. Rather our military might is composed of those who have voluntarily submitted to the rigors of defending freedom for all of America. Let there be no doubt that these are virtuous individuals. They place the needs and safety of their families and friends, ahead of their own. Each generation is allotted a small percentage of these incredible human beings. Our generation was no different.This is the story of a small group of Americans who volunteered to provide military service for their country. During that service they were unexpectedly thrust into a brutally difficult situation. Most of those that will pick up this book are completely unaware of this group of young men and women, and the honorable service that they performed. I suspect that even those family and friends of our team members are unaware of the extent to which those duties and the years following 9/11 affected the team. This is the story of the DERT Team that served in the Dover Port Mortuary following the events of September 11th, 2001. The acronym DERT stands for Dental Evidence Response Team. This story will be told from my first-hand account during those years and interviews with those team members closest to me in the following years. I've decided to not make up one detail. If my team or I could not remember the particulars of an incident, we didn't try to. We stuck to the facts, as we remembered. Of course we realize that sometimes history and time render facts fluid, and like written human history are always remembered and told from individual perspective. That is, there is another side to every story ever told.

While writing this book I was determined to document these events honestly, and to share them in an organized manner by timeline. Our reflections are heart-felt, and shared with a love for America's fallen heroes. Along with being honest in my recollections, another hope is that this book will provide some validation of the team's service and emotional closure for those team members. Should this book find its way into the hands of one of my old friends on that team, and you find error, please contact me directly and immediately. While reviewing my team member's interview notes it occurred to me that our team may not have remembered the entire journey exactly the same, but let there be no doubt that this entire manuscript is a journey of hope and love. I painted that path as honestly as I could, but in my experience I understand it is possible that some may take exception.

So this manuscript is going to take you on a journey into the heart of the military mortuary service worker from my perspective, with my team's influence and perspective included. In this case most of those folks will be forensic dental technicians. Those whom I speak of in this book are real people, were there on-station at Dover Air Force Base with me, and served on active duty alongside of me. Though at times it may seem like it, this is not just my story. This is our team's story, and there is no way I could have completed it without my team's ongoing love and support, and recollections of those early and traumatic days. This work is meant as personal documentation and validation of our team's tremendous duty of reuniting fallen American heroes with their families located all over the United States.

The story must come from my perspective, as it flows out of my interpretation of the interviews I shared with each of those members, and ultimately my own memories. I have made an attempt to describe the emotional trauma, the associated pain, and related and ongoing consequences of my years among the dead. Writing about personal trauma requires deep thought, reflection and is inherently difficult. It should never be rushed. All those I spoke with shared varying essential elements of their individual trauma and recovery. However, when describing specific incidents, I stayed in my own safe zone. Should any of my peers decide to come out later, and describe their own visions of trauma, I would be happy to assist them on their journeys. I accept all responsibility for this book's content. Every single word was written with love for my team, as well as the fallen heroes. It would be impossible to overstate the high regard in which I hold every single one of them.

Many of my personal recollections were shaky and confused. Not just because of the amount of time that has passed, but due to the fact that I spend most of my time consciously trying to not think about what happened. So you must wonder, if I'm really trying so hard to forget the past, why would I want to document it? Ultimately the answer to that question is the exact reason I am writing. This is a part of my life, and our team's life that has changed everything about us. It is not that we are better or worse, that could be argued until the end of time, but we are very different. As with all life lessons you can learn and grow or you can sit and stew in the struggle. Our team has chosen to be grateful for the incredible opportunity, and move on. This experience was a great life lesson for each of our team members, but for me personally it is time to close that chapter. It seems that most of our team agrees.

There are literally hundreds if not thousands of books written post-9/11. You could probably read a book every week for the rest of your life, and not be able to read every story. For me this one was very different, and this one was very personal. This story undeniably one of humans in service to others. All deaths are horrible to someone. We have all lost someone very close to us, and for a time following that death we were unsure if we would ever be able to move on. The grief process cannot be rushed, and we have fully accepted the very real probability that we never would be the same. I am not taking that from anyone, as it has also been my personal experience, yet I want to assure the team that in my experience time and distance have allowed for incredibly improved overall wellness.

A combat military death is different than other deaths, and creates an entirely different aura for all those connected with that death. Whether taking their last breath next to a buddy on the battlefield, lying on my cold hard steel table in the mortuary, or returned home in full service dress, the combat battlefield death is one of high reverence and respect. This is a soul removed from our society that was dedicated to providing freedom not just for you and I, but for our children and their children. This was another human being who understood that the democracy that we enjoy in this free American society must be continually nurtured. There are many in this world who would love to take our freedom away. This brother or sister in arms refused to let that happen. Indeed, they stood up for all of us. Now they were gone. This is a tremendous loss not only to their family and friends, but a tremendous loss for our entire society and each one of us. You do not have to believe me, agree with me, or recognize it, but these are the facts. Young men and women just like these fallen heroes are *the reason that we are able to speak out today*, and wake in the morning to a free and opportune life.

As you pour through this manuscript, *you should always remember*, that those who paid for our freedom with their lives, and their families are the true heroes of this mortuary tale. Parts of this story will be deeply and emotionally hurtful to any human souls that have decided to read it. You may believe some of my words to be too graphic, or unnecessary. But as previously described, violence is ultimately the essence of war, and should not be overlooked. Human beings die in war, and they die in horrific ways. War should be the last resort in resolving national problems, and if you take the time to digest this book, I suspect that you will agree with me. When speaking to a close friend during the preparation of this manuscript, he observed that every politician should be exposed to mortuary duty prior to committing the troops to war. I will not delve into political leanings in this work, but my dear friend proposes a valid argument.

Fifteen years are gone by, and it is critically important to me that the team's service during those years not be forgotten. Our service was honorable, and always with positive intention. During those years I did not personally witness one untoward action in the mortuary. One hundred percent of the time our fallen heroes' were treated with dignity, honor, and respect, with the primary goal of quickly and accurately returning the fallen heroes to their families. I served with a group that exemplified service before self. Regardless of the difficulty we faced, or the trauma that war had caused, I would not take back one single work day with that group of incredible Americans. I don't know if I can do the story justice, but you better believe that I am going to try.

The situation that our team, our family and friends, and our nation were placed in on 9/11 was unimaginable. The attack was unprovoked and directed on innocent civilians. It seems unlikely that any national intelligence service could have ever predicted the magnitude of that strike on our free nation. If anyone was aware of the possibility that our nation would be struck, no one in my small circle was aware of it. The day

before was little different than any other day in America during my lifetime. A couple of generations had passed since the
conflicts of the sixties, and twelve years had passed since the
end of the Cold War, and the fall of the Berlin Wall. Terrorism
certainly existed in the world, but it seemed unlikely to ever
be able to affect us so directly in our safe haven, isolated by
oceans, and enjoying nearly a century of American military
might. Discord in the Middle East, and the associated mal-
treatment of women and minorities in those countries, were
rarely thought of by the ordinary American. Even those most
demonstrative and determined to change unjust social conditions in America, seemed unaware or unconcerned with the
ongoing suffering of those directly in the path of Socialism, or
the Taliban, or any other third-world terrorists.

Just before the terrorists' attacks life appeared normal in
America. President Bush spent the morning before the attack
in Florida visiting schools, and promoting reading education.
As the Major League Baseball season wound down, the New
York Yankees enjoyed a 13-game lead over the Boston Red Sox
in the American League East, and the Dow Jones closed virtu-
ally unchanged at 9,605. The Monday Night Football game between the New York Giants and Denver Broncos ended well
after midnight on the East Coast. While some viewers dreaded
waking early to get back to work, some who worked in the
World Trade Center would soon be very thankful to arrive
late on 9/11. For me personally, September 10, 2011 was the
end of the first half of my life. I was completely unaware at the
time, but fifteen years later in retrospect there is no doubt in

my mind that my life will always be divided into two distinct halves. That is pre and post 9/11.

That day has directly influenced all areas of my life since, and I've accepted that it will always be that way. There simply is no going back. There has been a lot of healing in the years that have passed, and the hard days have become distinctly less anxious. Yet those images of life in the mortuary for the three weeks following the horror of those plane attacks on New York City and the Pentagon will never be forgotten. So how do I remember it, and how does the team that I shared those horrendous duties with remember it? Even more important, how have we gone on with our lives, and how are we doing today? That's what I want to document in this book, and hopefully it will help my ongoing healing, as well as those peers on my team who shared those duties with me.

I have been thinking about writing this book, and have been drafting notes on this project for many years. On the other hand, making the actual decision to complete what I had long ago started did require a commitment. It required not only reminiscing deep into past emotional pain, but many months in front of my laptop, physically organizing and documenting the facts of the story. Completing it meant research, and getting back into contact with that team that served alongside me in the mortuary. This completed work that you are reading was the most emotionally draining project that I have ever accomplished. Now with fifteen years gone by I want to acknowledge and share with the world how incredible each of my mortuary peers was, and that without the shared support of the team any one of us would have experienced a much more difficult journey.

The team was together in many senses, not just because of a shared background in the military, but placed into a moment of time that not any one of us could have imagined in our worst nightmares. It seems much more difficult looking back from a distance, and now realizing that those years were muddled in tremendous emotional pain and trauma. During those years, any one of the life decisions made by me or my team was influenced by the painful emotional trauma of our mortuary experience. I think it is important that we accept responsibility for any of our actions, forgive ourselves and others, and move forward with our lives. Though we maintain responsibility for those actions, today we have a much better understanding of the direction of our lives in those years.

During my mortuary time I was numb, and now I often wonder now how anyone on that team got out of that building with any semblance of emotional or mental health. The purpose of this disclosure is not to assign blame or regret to the military, or my unit, or my chain of command. To the contrary, I am certain our chain of command took every possible action to assist us, and even to protect us. We had each volunteered for this duty in the port mortuary. We may have suffered emotional consequences of that service, but we had accepted it willingly, and together we did survive that service with dignity and honor. Our team recognized that it was a tremendous privilege to serve America's fallen heroes. We were blessed to be there, destined to be there, even as our struggles with life, and our first-hand knowledge of death would impact the rest of our days on this lonely planet.

I did not contact every single individual that served in the mortuary with me over those years. I did attempt contact with my team mates who directly impacted my daily duties, and had an intimate understanding of the tremendous nightmare that the team suffered in those early years in the mortuary. Many I was able to speak to, though sadly some remain out of touch. The team we assembled, and the core group from those years was generally a seasoned bunch. By seasoned I mean a majority of us were well into our thirty-somethings, with a wide-range of life experiences, though limited mortuary experience. We did have our share of younger airman serving, with limited military and life experience. It was the younger team members that we worried about most. With less life experience to fall back on, the daily rigors of the mortuary was challenging at best. Regardless of age or experience we did have one thing in common. All team members were completely determined to serve our country, and motivated to contribute whenever and however we were needed. The team was hopeful, fun-loving, and dedicated to this wonderful nation. Without a doubt, they were and remain highly motivated patriots, and though they didn't go into combat, combat certainly did come to them.

This manuscript only reviews a very distinct portion of time. The reason for that is simply that these were the years that I was physically in the building, and I am able to provide factual accounts, albeit from my perspective. More importantly it should be noted, that from my perspective is exactly why I took the time to reach out to the others. I wanted to make sure I was remembering some of the details and specific accounts of those years accurately. It also should be noted, and always remembered that there were many other mortuary teams and contingencies long before our team arrived, and others long after our departure. I know that this book will find its way into the hands of some of these incredible past, present and future mortuary service-workers. I spoke to less than two dozen of those who came before or after, but their recollection and sentiment is similar to mine. The story of our team is familiar to their memories of service. Their reactions and experiences to the trauma may have been more or less severe, but we share a very similar remembrance of our days in the port mortuary. All that served in the mortuary are incredibly proud of that service, and they have every right to feel that way. I hope and pray that anyone who stepped foot inside that building to serve, whether for one day, of ten years will understand and believe that they have my undying love and respect. Every single one of them is an American hero.

The events of 9/11, and the years of mortuary service shifted my deep-held world view that inside of our nations' borders our families and friends were safe. Suddenly I realized that this was not true. Those planes could have been crashed into any building on the east coast, or in fact, anywhere in America. Flight 93 crashed in Shanksville, Pennsylvania which is very near my childhood home. How many millions of people were in very near proximity of those strikes in New York City and Washington, D.C? When those planes hit, it was reasonable to consider that other strikes were imminent. Many of those I was serving with at the time of the strike reported very similar thoughts. I suspect much of America felt the same way. For the first time in our lives Americans had good reason to be fearful for their safety. This realization immediately changed thought patterns for many in our nation. Even today, how many people around the world continue to live their lives in a chronic state of such fear? The answer is millions. While here in America we have returned to our internal bickering and politicking, rather than remaining grateful for the freedom we enjoy.

Time has a funny way of going on with or without your consent. Moments turn into days, which turn into years. Our lives quietly slip away, and we only have control over our immediate and individual personal actions. The future is unknown. Who could have ever known what the future held for America and specifically our small band of Airman at Dover AFB on September 10th, 2001? Prior to 9/11 I was well-adjusted, outgoing, and always seeking a positive outcome to any difficult life situation. I had been in the military for over fifteen years, and had thrived over four military assignments. I arrived at Dover Air Force Base in the spring of 2001 with the expectation to finish my twenty years at Dover, and return to my civilian life. I was happy to be back on the East Coast, and especially happy to learn that I had friends already on station.

The Air Force is a small community, and it seems whenever you land at a new assignment anywhere in the world, you have a built in history with some folks already on your new station. If you are in the military, this is good reason to treat others kindly and with compassion, as you will probably see them again. In this case, I'd been reunited with multiple friends, including one who had served with, and trained me in my first assignment at Wright-Patterson AFB, Ohio. He immediately made me feel welcome. The dental clinic was small, with about thirty active duty assigned, and the group was very supportive of one another. As a part of the larger command this clinic was a bit different than the other dental flights around the military. This particular clinic in central Delaware was part of the base mortuary mission of forensic identification. Dover Air Force Base maintains the military's only port mortuary. I understood this upon arrival, and was excited to be a part of such a challenging mission.

Forensic identification is a critical component of the military process of serving our fallen heroes. Depending on circumstance of the human remains, forensic dental identifications are often the quickest and most accurate methods of making a positive identification. On human remains that have suffered disfigurement, fragmentation, or have been burnt beyond recognition, the teeth with its enamel usually survive. That's where the dental forensic technician would step in. Physically, the jaw would be opened to reveal remaining dentition and to be radiographed. Anyone who has ever served in the military understands that dental appointments are a routine part of military service. Unlike our civilian counterparts, the military dental examination is a mandatory appointment. The initial dental examinations in basic military training (boot camp) are where every entering service member receives a panoramic radiograph. A film of this type displays full dentition of the upper and lower jaws. This film then follows the service member for the remainder of their time on active duty, and if ever needed could easily be compared to films taken post-mortem. In the hands of a trained forensic dentist, this could make for a quick and accurate identification regardless of the condition of the body.

It's very easy to get lost in the gruesome details of mortuary duty, and to feel sorry for ourselves or our team. But, that's not what our team was about; not how we felt about the duty then, and not how we feel now. Our duty was a service of love, and we should always remember and celebrate this service. We should remember that it was not just our feelings, or our personal lives that were shattered and changed forever. We went through this tragedy as a nation. A decade and a half has passed and my feelings along with those with whom I served continue to suffer. Today I am better, and the team is better, yet the traumas of that endless flow of the human remains of our very own American heroes will affect us until the end of time.

Generations are affected by war. This has been true throughout recorded history, and I suspect it was true even before human beings began documenting their lives with written symbols or words. As has always been, every single deceased war hero has a story, and each of those deaths will affect their families for multiple generations that follow. I hope the families of those who came through Dover, and read this story will understand that every single service-member working in that mortuary treated each American casualty as a brother or sister. In our hearts we understood that these heroes could have very well been anyone of us.

Our team was just like the victims. We were young, physically strong, and ambitious. We were hopeful for improving the world. We were dreamers, and rather than just having this dream, we took action. There is a huge difference in those that think about doing something, and those that actually do.

We knew the difference. We took ourselves down to the local recruiting station, signed up, and then preceded to the military entrance processing station (MEPS). Each military member raises their right hand and took an oath to defend the freedoms that this country enjoys. Those that passed through that mortuary on gurneys were indeed our brothers and sisters, and we loved them as we loved our own families. We understood their sacrifice for an ideal much greater than themselves. I can think of no offering a human being on this planet could make, than to lay down their life, for their fellow citizens freedom.

Our team will never forget those moments we shared among the dead. Each of us has needed time and space for our individual thoughts and feelings. But one reality remains. Sooner or later we each had to directly face the realities of those days we spent in the port mortuary. Most made the attempt not to think about it at all. Actually, we were probably each guilty of that sentiment, at least for some time. Eventually those memories must be confronted. Some told me they felt fine, and had compartmentalized those feelings. One even said she used an internal button, and could turn the memories and feelings on and off. She said this was necessary because it was impossible to be able to tell others about those days in the mortuary. I felt and understood the joy in her voice speaking to me, as I understood exactly what she was sharing, and she knew that I knew. This is a wonderful gift and one of my most precious discoveries over the past year speaking to my old teammates. We can still help each other. Together our team did the absolute best we could for as long as we could, and served those who could no longer serve themselves. Now,

I want to assure each of my fellow team members, that it is time to heal.

This is a slice my teams' lives and military service that must be documented and remembered. I first sat down to write about this experience immediately following 9/11. In those early days, it was not meant to be, but I did maintain my notes. A few years later I started again, but just could not face the memories and the trauma. I found it impossible to put some of those most hurtful memories into words, but my dream of writing about this journey never wavered. As the years have gone by, I've been able to step back a little and think about the bigger picture. I was in such a deep pain for so long; the shroud of that trauma is only now beginning to recede. Once I started writing, the story flowed especially with the support of my peers. Talking to them was pure joy, and hearing their thoughts and their remembrances sped this entire process.

This is an incredible story, of an incredible team and their military service, but the story of our team in this book can only review the time that I was personally stationed at the mortuary, from 9/11 until 2006. Further, my first-hand knowledge can only include those duties of the DERT Team. Even my first-hand knowledge may be flawed in some detail. I have directly spoken too many of those who personally shared the duty with me. During this year, I've sometimes found it difficult to translate their absolute memories. I promise I have tried hard to convey their message, as it is ingrained with my own. It is interesting to start to think about the past, and try to remember what happened. Your reality is going to be different than mine, even if we spent the majority of the time serving together.

I am certain that my team shared their truths with me, even when I couldn't remember an incident that they shared. It would be impossible for me to reveal truths from those circumstances of which I can barely remember, may not have remembered in the same way, or in some cases may not have remembered at all. If I've slighted anyone on my team, I'm dreadfully sorry, and they should know that above all, they each will have my lifetime love and respect. Some have not been named out of their own wishes, and a few I was unable to locate, but all are remembered. I would do anything in my power to assist any one of them. I am terribly proud of every single member of that team. I hope that each reader will find hope, and feel love for the DERT Team journey during those early years at Dover Air Force Base, after that horrible day that changed America.

3

DOVER AIR FORCE BASE

Time spent anywhere is a valuable opportunity to learn from your world. Such was the case with the tiny, yet prominent state of Delaware. So inconspicuous in size, often lost in the conversation when discussing history, geography, or political science. Yet, my experiences in the First State, changed my perception of the entire world. Friends that I met sharing the same time and spaces with in Delaware are those same friends that will forever remain in my heart. Do not underestimate the significance of wherever you are today. For my active military friends, do not complain about your assignment, embrace it. Though you don't believe me now, I promise you will look back with fond memories.Dover is the capital of the First U.S. State of Delaware. It is also Delaware's second largest city. It is located along the St. Jones River in the Delaware River coastal plain, and was founded in 1683 by William Penn. The old city's central square is known as The Green and to this day is the central location of many patriotic events held by the city. Dover is also the home of the famed American Revolution wartime leader Caesar Rodney. He is buried in the surrounding area, although the precise location is unknown. A cenotaph in his honor is erected at the Episcopal Church near The Green.

On December 7th, 1787, at the Golden Fleece Tavern on The Green, the legislature of Delaware ratified the United States Constitution, and Delaware thus became "The First State." Today you can see the historic plaque prominently displayed along the quaint and brick-lined South State Street, or enjoy a tour of the historic district. It is not unusual to enjoy a period-dressed entertainer strolling The Green and sharing a colonial education with visitors. However, if you ask one of the local military troops about The Golden Fleece, they'll most likely point you to a local bar just a couple of blocks away on Loockerman Street. Being a lifelong bachelor and a military man himself, I doubt Caesar Rodney would disapprove. Dover Air Force Base is also located near here, sitting just about two miles southeast of the historic downtown area.

Dover's original airfield was converted to an Army Air Corps airfield just weeks after the Japanese air attack on Pearl Harbor in December 1941. With the establishment of the United States Air Force on September 18th, 1947, the facility was renamed Dover Air Force Base on January 13th, 1948. The base remained a stalwart community fixture, employing thousands of local civilians and pumping life into the most eastern shore's economy ever since. In 1973, Dover became the first all C-5 equipped air wing in the U.S. Air Force, and was subsequently named one of only seven airports in the country that served as a launch abort facility for the Space Shuttle.

The United States Air Force has operated the C-5 Galaxy, one of the largest aircraft in the world, since 1969. The cargo hold of the massive C-5 is one foot longer than the entire length of the first powered flight by the Wright Brothers at Kitty Hawk, North Carolina. The Galaxy aircraft is capable of moving six Boeing AH-64 Apache helicopters or five Bradley Fighting Vehicles at one time. Since its introduction, this heavy airlifter has supported American military operations in all major conflicts including Vietnam, Iraq, Yugoslavia and Afghanistan, as well as allied support to, and including Israel during the Yom Kippur War and contingent operations in the Gulf War. The Galaxy has also been used to distribute humanitarian aid and disaster relief, and has as mentioned above supported the United States Space Shuttle program.

Following the attacks of September 11th, 2001, the 436th Air Wing and 512th Reserve Air Wing became major contributors to the missions of Operation Enduring Freedom and Operation Iraqi Freedom. An aircrew from Dover's 3rd Airlift Squadron landed the first C-5 in Iraq in late 2003 at Baghdad International Airport. Also, and more pertinently to this manuscript, following 9/11, mortuary specialists at the Dover Air Force Base Port Mortuary began organizing for direct support of the Pentagon recovery effort.

The tragic events of September 11, 2001 resulted in over 3,000 human beings murdered in terrorist attacks. Incredibly, these atrocities occurred on American soil and all within a few hours' drive of the small military base in Dover where I was currently assigned to duty. The primary attack on the World Trade Centers was not just an attack on our nation, but an attack on the free world. New York City is recognized as the crossroads of the world and the gleaming hope of freedom for millions of foreigners who will never set foot on our shores. You would be hard-pressed to spend any time on the streets of Seoul, London or Tokyo and not see a New York Yankees baseball cap. Tragedy not only directly impacted our largest city, but also Washington, DC, the capital of this freedom-loving nation. It was not a coincidence that those cities were struck.

On that day, our free, democratic society suffered a destructive blow through the deeds of pure evil. September 11th saw those dark forces stand up and challenge our faith in all that is good in our open democracy. There could no longer be any doubt among our free and loving people that this evil exists. The days following 9/11 are days filled with pain, suffering, and misery. It hurt many of us, scarring our souls, and searing our memories with previously unimaginable thoughts. That day destroyed the very foundation of our innate belief that we were safe. Suddenly we weren't. During this time of trial, many heroes emerged. Those citizens who were determined to find hope in fellow Americans through a deep and unshaken faith in their Higher Power. God helped the believers to close ranks and muster the strength to never give up, and to ultimately move forward.

Piles of rubble were being excavated and broadcast daily on the cable news, as we watched policemen, firemen, and volunteers search for survivors. We re-lived stories of the attack, stories of those who rushed into harm's way to help, and witnessed many of those heroes sacrifice their lives to save others. Broadcast on live television, we witnessed grief beyond belief as those burning souls a hundred stories above street level leapt out of this world, and to their sure death. All horrible and sometimes incredible stories full of Americans placed in unheard of circumstances. We saw personal stories of kindness amidst the disaster, watching and hearing about ordinary people doing incredible and extraordinary things for their neighbors. Differences in culture and belief were set aside. Our nation came together as one, and amidst the pain maintained faith and hope in our world. Those early days were surreal for all of America, and the reality of that despair was no different in our little corner of the world in Dover.

Disasters such as these tend to lock our memories into place. Over the years I often heard stories of where family or friends had been, and what they had been doing, when breaking news reported the assassination of President Kennedy on that sunny afternoon in Dallas in November of 1963. Or where they had been sitting, and thinking when that little black and white television set shared the news that man had landed on the moon. Back then, everyone had to step outside, and look up wondering if it were true. Such was the case with September 11th. What I have since discovered is that those locked-in memories are not as certain as I thought. There is always margin for error, and human beings tend to remember facts differently. This is not good or bad, it just is.

On the morning of September 11th, most of our team remembered sitting with other staff in our Clinic's waiting area watching in disbelief as the second plane hit the tower, and the subsequent disasters at the Pentagon and in Western Pennsylvania. As earlier described, the history of Dover Air Force Base in central Delaware is a long and distinguished one. Though small in size, with a shape mirroring the flight line, the base contains a major airlift hub supporting worldwide excursions in wartime and peace. At the time of my arrival thirty-some of the monstrous C-5 Galaxy's were parked out on the military runway. The C-5 is one of the world's largest airplanes, and a few dozen sitting in line were not only a spectacular sight, but also a tempting target. One quick blow by an enemy could remove a large percentage of our nation's airlift capabilities. While we may or may not have been on the terrorist's radar, the thought of this potential calamity certainly did not escape our thoughts.

In addition, the base contains the military's only port mortuary. It also is one of the largest such facilities in the world. The mortuary is staffed by a diverse array of professionals from numerous federal agencies, along with active and reserve personnel from all military services. A book could surely be written on the history of this facility, and any feeble remarks by me to serve it historical justice will fall short. So rather than attempting, I will keep my eye on the ball and my focus on a very small and distinct group of airmen. This was a group of ordinary Americans who found themselves together facing terrible tragedy and discovering that together, as a team, they could persevere and accomplish their duties.

Moments after the second plane struck the World Trade Center (WTC), and for the first time in my military career, the entire air base was placed into real-world Condition Delta. This meant that all base gates were locked and base personnel were frozen in place. This was not an exercise, and we all knew it. Military Humvee vehicles were parked at the air base main gate and manned with live 50-caliber machine guns. All around the base folks were anxious. Not just for ourselves, but for what this meant for our family, our friends, and our nation. Doors to base buildings and all hospital clinics were locked as our staff remained in stunned silence. While I had been at Dover for less than a year, I along with the other staff understood that this disaster would soon directly impact our daily lives. Even before the Pentagon was hit later in the morning we realized that the port mortuary would most likely soon be filled with the tragic aftermath of what was unfolding in front of us on live cable television. That meant we needed to prepare. Leadership in the clinic called the staff together, confirmed our fears and laid out a plan of preparation. Immediately we would begin the extensive legwork completing the administrative side of mortuary contingency preparations. Additional manning needed secured, chains of command needed briefing, and the dental clinic needed to get emotionally and physically prepared. More critically, we had to do it quickly and accurately.

Next door to us the main hospital building was also immediately placed into internal lockdown, with no souls coming in, and no souls going out. If you've never been on a military base, the physical layout of the buildings is much like that of your average American town. There are differences of course. Each building is identified with a number, and the exact purpose

of that building is stated on a well-maintained and easily dis-
cernable government-issue brown sign. Generally speaking
those numbers were ascending and descending, and tracking a
specific target would have been easily done. Should someone
from the outside be looking to create havoc on such a facility,
they certainly could find access to specific units, and probably
specific staff. I'm not sure this was well thought out prior to
the 9/11 incident, but we certainly thought of it afterwards.

Clinic personnel immediately covered all outside identifying signs and blocked the windows with brown wrapping
paper. No peering out and no peering in. Outside of the
building movement was limited. We needed permission to
depart our station, and then only for specific need. If an
airman had been working outside on the air base or maybe
the flight line, with no communications shortly after this
lockdown, they surely would have wondered what was happening. We ran an internal call roster base-wide, and soon
the staff was accounted for. Those on leave were not getting
on the base, and were advised to remain in place, and maintain contact with their supervisors. Those same checklists
that were being reviewed on our base were most likely being followed at every American military base stateside, as
well as overseas. For the first time in our team's lives and
our military service, the American homeland was under attack, and in those early moments, none of us understood
the repercussions of that attack, or what our nation would
soon face.

The medical clinics cancelled all appointments, and we
had stand-by care retirees locked into the clinic with us. We

were all trying to reach out by telephone to families, but the phone lines were jammed, overwhelmed and not operating. The young mothers in our clinic were very worried about their small children. By mid-afternoon those concerned mothers were granted permission to walk to the nearby childcare facility and return their children to our now bunkered clinic. Other staff scurried around in preparation, and a few stayed near the television watching the incredible newscast. All chatting with one another, and wondering what this attack meant. America was at war? Each of us was now faced with the reality of impending wartime service. What would that mean, and how would it affect the remainder of our lives, and the lives of our family and friends?

On the information systems side our team was working diligently to bring the future of positive forensic dental identification into the here and now. The subsequent buildup of hardware and technology allowed our clinic to achieve the unthinkable. Indeed, in very short order the systems effort led by Daniel Hines stood up the capability and further executed the technology becoming the first forensic dental team in history to attempt to fully utilize digital dental radiology in a mass disaster response. The technology previously existed, but this would be the first attempt to use it under mass casualty conditions.

This was a noteworthy leap in technology as it meant that dental radiographs could be executed and viewed accurately in real time. Additionally, they could quickly be re-accomplished if necessary. With the digital forensics capability on site, the forensic dentist could easily be within view of the screen and request any variation of the presented radiograph. There is no doubt that achieving this feat for the 9/11 disaster was not only a tremendous benefit to the entire team, but an incredible advance for our nation. In the past, dental radiographs were taken using hard films. These films were then taken into dark-rooms, and then developed chemically in a film processor. This wet process was not only time consuming, but the quality was not consistent. Digital was a whole new ballgame, and while the team welcomed it, there certainly was some concern. Could we meet this challenge?

Due to this trepidation, Jennifer Jones was on the telephone, and busy calling local-area civilian dental clinics requesting donations of radiographic film. We all wanted to believe the "new" digital dental technology would be effective, but were certainly not going to go into this huge contingency without a back-up plan. Jennifer had a quick, easy and professional rapport, and reported incredible response from the local community as many downtown dental facilities offered to donate their civilian services and supplies. Fortunately for our team and our nation, those donations would never be needed, as our digital effort would ultimately prove successful.

On the medical logistics side Edward Anderson was inventorying bulk medical goods, and working feverishly to obtain the dental supplies that would be required for this massive contingency. He was a seasoned logistics professional, and quite adept at securing any necessary medical or other non-medical requirements. Along with this knowledge, he had already been involved with multiple critical incidents and probably brought the most hands-on experience to the current team. Early on the team leaned on him heavily, and he never disappointed. He took the time and patience to share and teach. No matter how many radiographs a dental technician had taken in his career, preparing for and executing radiographs on human remains is quite a different endeavor.

Besides the emotionality of being in such intimate proximity to the deceased, the smell and the sight, there was the functional difficulty of maneuvering the jaws into position for an accurate radiograph. While we may have talked to the human remains to encourage cooperation, it was always technique that accomplished the job. So Ed played a very key role in the training of our technicians. If any of us were unable to get the shot correctly, Ed was there. Aside from these strengths, he was compassionate and empathetic. In my years working with him under the most unimaginably difficult of circumstances, I never once witnessed him upset or heard him raise his voice. Under these incredible stressful conditions, his sense of calm was powerful, and was a tremendous force in keeping the dental forensics team grounded.

Greg McCulley was developing a shift schedule, and helping to prepare the mortuaries dental area for its largest forensics contingency in many years. The dental clinic at Dover was not a large clinic. We may have had eight or nine dental officers, and a couple of dozen technicians. But not all of those technicians were available for mortuary service. Working with the dead had to be voluntary, and we started with all available hands during those three weeks after 9/11. About a dozen enlisted rotated through those three weeks; seven days a week, and twelve to fourteen hours per day. What I soon learned was that those who came to the mortuary to assist were completely dedicated to this difficult mission. Getting them to take shifts was never a problem during those early weeks. The problem was getting them to go home and rest.

Along with Ed, another of the key dental radiology technicians during those early days was Stephen Sedlock. Looking back over my military career, there were those fellow service members that I liked a lot, and then there was a small percentage that I loved. Steve was in the latter category. If I were assigned any forensics or mortuary mission, Steve would be my first choice to assist. He was always smiling and incredibly bright. He kept any environment positive by bringing joy and light to our service, plus he was a natural at taking radiographs. Of course all dental technicians were adept with the proper techniques and procedures during technical training, but he had transcended all proper method. He not only would accept the most difficult tasking's, but he would always provide accurate and timely products. Aside from this, he was a joy to be around. Most importantly, he further cemented the core of our team, and his warm demeanor always kept the group upbeat and hopeful.

In the face of this disaster the team stayed positive, and was determined to get the job done. I always share this story for the old Air Force folks, because I know they would appreciate it. Having served in the military for over twenty-one years I have read many hundreds of annual performance reports. It seems 90% of every enlisted performance report I have ever seen, including my own, said the airman has a can-do attitude. Well, this team had that can-do attitude in aces.

And they were always willing to share it. This was a team of leaders, and any single one of us was capable of stepping up to lead as necessary. This is what allowed our team to succeed. We trusted and respected one another, and allowed all those volunteers who came into contact with our team the motivation to help support us. This further allowed our team the freedom to successfully complete the duty. These traits would become more valuable as time passed, though at the time we had no idea of what our futures held.

Late on the afternoon of 9/11, the reality of the disaster had come into focus, as we learned that human remains would be arriving on Dover, from the Pentagon disaster by early morning. The images from that day's television broadcasts were stunning, as if not a part of our world in the United States. It seemed to be a third world disaster, or an attack somewhere in the Middle East. We had burning towers, with crashing debris, and bodies buried deep in that steel pile of rubble. The day was almost a dream, a horrendous nightmare, disturbing each of our lives in the most personal and devastating of ways. Each team member slowly or quickly had to come to terms with this new reality, and to take that reality home to our families and friends. Putting it into perspective or making sense out of this terrible dream was impossible. All we could do was react to our impending duties, and prepare as best we could. Our wartime mission was now officially underway.

Most of us by now had been able to text or speak with our families. I lived on base, but we were separated from the main base by a state highway. My family lived in base housing just a few doors down from the middle school where our son

attended. I knew my family was home and were safe, but naturally I remained concerned about their wellness. The team was
released that evening around 6 P.M. and all were advised to get
as much rest as possible as the next few weeks would surely be
filled with long and difficult duty. Those evening hours were
spent re-watching the tragedy on our cable television, with estimates of the dead seeming to increase with each broadcast
that evening. The goal was to disconnect from the day's horrid
events, and get some sleep, but that was not the reality. Early
evening quickly turned into late night, and the alarm clock
rang early. Each of our team members would arise and charge
into an unfamiliar and disturbing brand-new world.

The following three weeks would find the team locked
into the old mortuary building, which stood on Dover Air
Force Base near the south end of the flight line, on grounds
today occupied by the new Charles C. Carson Port Mortuary.
The old mortuary building could most accurately be described as spacious and open; the walls were olive drab and
tent-like, canvas, or tarp, with large rickety-rackety fans
hanging clumsily from the ceiling. Mobile partitions and
panels divided the work areas, minimally providing some
sense of seclusion for those trying to concentrate on any
present duties. There were also multiple industrial-strength
bug-zappers in the building in an ongoing attempt to contain the flies that were drawn to the unmistakable fragrance
of decaying human remains. The smell was permanent, regardless of whether or not the building was being utilized.
The heating and cooling units were inadequate for the size
of the facility. If you were working you were freezing or

sweating, and that fine line of time with perfect weather never seemed to seep into the facility.

Despite our ongoing efforts to maintain a neat and clean environment, the concrete floors, walls, and even equipment were blood-stained with years of use. Any bleach-motivated attempts to remove those stains were futile. The building was naturally dark, with limited or essentially ineffective lighting. Flies were omnipresent, and swatting at them an exercise in futility. The bug-zappers were just as useless. If a third-rate nightmarish movie were ever produced about those early days, it would be impossible to overstate the dread with which that old mortuary resounded.

Regardless of the mortuary's physical shortcomings, that antiquated building resonated with history, tradition and service. To this day when talking with some of the past mortuary workers their memories are skewed to the positive. Human memories work in funny ways, we remember what we choose to recall, and throw out the rest. Incredible duties were completed, and contingencies never forgotten. The original mortuary had been used beginning in 1955, and would close in 2003. It had been used to identify and process the remains of an estimated 50,000 military service members. It also was utilized in 1978 for the victims of the Jonestown mass murder-suicide, in 1986 for identifying the remains of the crew of the Space Shuttle Challenger and in 2003 for the crew of the Space Shuttle Columbia. On this proud and historic air base, this remnant make-shift building held its own. And though the port mortuary would again be challenged, again it would answer the call, and serve its nation proudly.

On Wednesday morning, September 12th, 2001 our team arrived at that old building to survey our inventory, and prepare to receive the remains from Flight 77 and the Pentagon attack. Three of us arrived very early, sometime just before 5 AM, and found few others in the building. The entrance and administrative area was staffed, but when we stepped into the back working area the lights hadn't even been turned on. Ed was two steps in front of me and flipped the switch, turned back to me and calmly said, "Let's get this done." Steve and I followed, and the other dental and mortuary staff workers joined us shortly after.

4

FLIGHT 77 & THE PENTAGON DISASTER

Tragedy is bound to intersect with each of our lives on this planet. Ultimately, that tragedy does not define who we are, or where we are going. What defines us is how we react to that tragedy. Such was the case with 9/11. Our world was changed, and done so beyond our control, under incredibly horrific conditions. We lost much, but what did we allow ourselves to gain? Allow yourself that opportunity to grow and learn from the struggles in your life.

Prior to 9/11 and the Pentagon disaster, a direct attack on American soil seemed impossible, yet it wasn't. And all of America had witnessed the homeland's vulnerability first-hand. Our free and open society with its welcoming and trustful history was again betrayed. Many noted these events as our generation's Pearl Harbor. Following the 9/11 strike on our freedom, our military team, along with hundreds of other professionals, was immediately faced with a wartime mission. Let me remind you again, because it is very important, this story is not meant to be a comprehensive view of the entire port mortuary and its service following 9/11. Even on the dental side of the effort there are names and faces long since forgotten. Talking to the mortuary team over the past year they have very fond memories of those sent temporary duty to Dover to provide assistance. And while I may not single them out in this book, we greatly appreciated their service. We had invaluable assistance from numerous military units, including Andrews, Langley, and Keesler Air Force bases; along with a group of forensic dentists from the Armed Forces Institute of Pathology in Washington, D.C. Together we blended our services and our talents, always looking to protect our fellow teammates while completing our duties. From the very beginning, the team understood what our tasking was, and that mission is what we focused on.

The days following saw Dover's historic and storied mortuary building quickly come to life once again. Soon the dining and break area was filled by the United Services Organization (USO) with a wide assortment of drinks, snacks and sundries. The local McDonald's provided breakfast biscuits, and coffee was consumed by the gallon. The small community that was Dover Air Force Base soon became a frantic hub of activity, and the staff was overwhelmed with empathy, compassion and care. It seemed the entire local community wanted to assist our service, and all on base genuinely appreciated the care and concern. While there is not one doubt that we would have successfully completed the mission without the support of the local community, it was wonderful to know that they were there. Dover should be very proud of its long military heritage and associated civilian community.

The port mortuary soon swarmed with the FBI, OSI, and NCIS, along with numerous other universally recognized units such as AFIP, and OAFME, the armed forces medical examiners. While the building screamed back to life in all sections, our small dental team retreated to our corner of this historic structure to prepare for the incoming human remains. Our dental team arrived at this contingency with minimal mortuary service. The year prior to September 11th the Dover Air Force Base dental clinic had undergone a transition in leadership, and senior enlisted personnel. The dental identification team had lost five individuals who previously had combined for nearly fifty years of service in the mortuary. This older team was outstanding in setting us up for success, and our team's accomplishments were built on those past years of dedication to the mission.

Time continues to pass, and the mission must always be completed, even if we were a bit green. Though I understood that my military orders to Dover would likely result in forensic mortuary work, I hadn't anticipated the possibility of a tragedy of this dimension, or the possibility of war. Though a declaration of war had not yet been issued by the United States, there was little doubt in any of our minds that America would reciprocate for this tragedy. We talked about the lessons of Pearl Harbor leading into WWII, and our concerns grew even greater. Most of us had friends and family serving in other branches of the military, including the Army and

Marine Corps. Would they be deployed once the investigation was complete? Maybe they were already in route into harm's way, and we'd be learning of those efforts later tonight, if we ever got home?

The majority of military members are universally, culturally and historically engaged. We pay attention to current events, as they may directly affect our lives. Among ourselves we are quick to share opinions, for better or worse. Off the record, of course. Surrounded by the dead, our talk often turned philosophical and led into a discussion of trying to understand the origins of evil and hate. Evil is psychiatrically defined as lack of empathy. Our team argued many things over our years together. However, there could be no denying that purposefully flying planeloads of innocent human beings into those towers in New York City full of innocent civilians showed a distinct lack of empathy. Indeed, whoever made this strike against our freedom was evil. What was it about our free lives that made them hate us so much?

For the majority of Americans, granting freedom to others in our American society seems humanly rational and humane, no matter how you reason it out in your mind, and no matter which side of the political spectrum you reside. Americans grow up free, and that freedom has allowed for a creativity of purpose that has furthered the cause of not just our own nation, but rather all of humanity. Much of the world looks toward the United States for leadership, though it should be noted, that there are other cultures around the world that consider us infidels for granting equal rights to all. This meant that whoever struck us was thinking in very different ways than we were. In fact it seems there is no way we could ever understand the other side's deepest held beliefs, as they may never understand ours. Yet, the outcome of those beliefs was now in our midst. America would soon become even more aware of her differences from those in the Middle East, and those differences may well affect all of our lives for a very long time.

Many of those differences were then and remain today substantial. Not only are the specific religious aspects different, but even more so in how we regard our treatment of others, and a distinct lack of tolerance. So why does America continue to try to blend cultures, and if we do, can other views be respected without diminishing the other? Are the differences in these cultural beliefs beneficial to either side, or both? There were so many questions and concerns, and so very few answers. But for now those questions would have to wait. For now, it was time for our team to concentrate on our task at hand, and regardless of our differences of opinion, our primary mission was to function together as one. And so we did.

Early on the morning of September 12th the entire team received a crash course in digital dental radiology from Daniel Hines. This included the use and placement of a digital sensor. This sensor was much less forgiving than normal dental film, in that it was extremely rigid. This made placement inside the mouth and at the gum line much more difficult as the anatomy of the mouth is defined by very hard structures. The enamel of the teeth is the hardest surface in a human body, and the mandible and maxilla are similarly immobile. The tongue muscle is pliable, but takes up much space, and in a small mouth the room to maneuver the dental sensor was minimal.

With the traditional dental film, we were able to flex the film to make it fit, not so now. However, using regular film, dipping into chemicals for exposure, and running through the film dryer all takes time. Should there be an improper dental shot performed, then a requirement for a re-take, it would have doubled the amount of the team's exposure to radiation. So the initial reviews were mixed. There also was the technological aspect of what we were doing. It's hard to imagine but those were the days with limited smart phones, or at least not like we enjoy today, and the idea of digital-anything was a foreign concept to a majority of those working among us. This was technology on a mass scale being implemented for the very first time in military or civilian dental history, and our learning curve was steep, and required an open mind.

Rather than being completely comfortable with what needed to be done, and how we were going to do it, we had to accept that we were going into a massive contingency and would be using a system none of us had ever seen or worked with. This little detail did not impede the team. Indeed, Dan was a highly motivated instructor, technologically ahead of his time, and his presence and experience at this moment in our shared history was invaluable. Our team was up for the challenge. Dan was our chief advocate and cheerleader, and his ability to share the knowledge and techniques of this brand-new digital technology allowed our team to exceed the challenge we were faced with. When talking to the team now, all agree that without the digital technology our services would have immensely suffered. While we were capable of completing the tasking of dental identification in the traditional way with wet dental film, it would have created a much more difficult task. With digital radiology and Dan's leadership our timeline for completion of this contingency was certainly cut in half. This allowed the team members less exposure to the demands of performing our mortuary duties. Further, our ultimate success on this mission quickly increased morale with the team, and would ultimately prepare us for larger demands of mortuary forensic service in the very near future.

Soon, large double-propped, camouflaged military helicopters began to arrive in Dover ferrying in the human remains from the Pentagon. The whump, whump, whumping soon became a nauseous sound and remains a trigger for many of the team even today. Over those next few weeks following 9/11 whether or not we were in the mortuary, we knew exactly what that sound meant. It meant the arrival of not only those military and civilian personnel killed while working quietly at their desks in the Pentagon, but also those souls aboard American Airlines Flight 77 destined for destruction. In Dover, body bags began to spill out of the sky aboard those massive choppers and were opened to reveal our greatest nightmare. The devastation that a day earlier had only been an eerie nightmare on cable television was now fully among us.

Those earliest shocking hours in that old mortuary are eternally burned into the minds of me and our entire team. Black body bags seemed to be piled into any and every empty space. We were literally surrounded by death; our living and breathing team members shuffled around, and their faces were overwhelmingly distraught with grief. The team bumped all over one another in the tight spaces of that old mortuary, stumbling around while continually executing the mission. I was working within a foot of my teammates, but staring into their eyes I knew they were already gone, mentally and emotionally checked out of this current time and space. All on station at the mortuary in that moment were in survival mode. It did not impede the team's progress. On a bathroom break looking into the mirror I realized my face revealed the same lost stare. I wasn't sure what I was looking for or looking at, but I knew something was wrong. Something in my eyes was already changed, and I barely recognized the glassy eyes, and glazed look. The moments turned into ten minutes, and one of my teammates came to check on me. I remember the hand on my shoulder, a quick chill, and then back to the realization of what we were doing. We didn't talk; it was too horrible to talk about. We just returned to our stations and kept working.

Probably everyone thinks about death at some time in their lives, but being confronted with it on a scale of this magnitude hurts one's soul, deeply, desperately, and intimately. These were not just ordinary deaths one accepts with a fully-lived, aged life. Rather this was the death of lives cut short, with dreams terminated instantly, leaving families grappling with the pain of a hole in their soul that can never be filled. The dead lay quietly. And they lay everywhere. There was no place to turn for a safe view from the trauma, we were surrounded. The body bags were opened and closed, and lined up on metal gurneys that seemed to overwhelm the building. The old building was large and open, but was now over-swollen with the past lives of those who could no longer speak for themselves. It's hard to describe being surrounded by death in this way. We have all walked through cemeteries which are full of the dead, but this was an unnatural and horrendous situation. While we all wanted to comfort the dead, comfort was not possible. We were stuck in two different worlds, and there would be no changing that fact. Those of us privileged, indeed blessed, to assist identify them did so diligently and with dignity.

Just a few days before the dead had been like us. They were living, breathing, warm and fleshy human beings, full of hope, dreams and desire wanting only to share life and love with their families and friends. They had just enjoyed the previous weekend, maybe seeing a movie or going out to eat with their spouse. Some were young, some a bit older, but all were now gone. The face of death is a million different faces, but still all the same. The human remains rested peacefully on the gurneys, some with eyes open staring into the void, glassy and looking directly at our team. I wondered if the Pentagon victims knew, if there were any warning at all, or God forbid those poor souls on the airplane. They knew for sure. The plane was coming down, not destined for a safe landing, and the passengers were all going down with it. Some had been able to make quick, final good-bye phone calls to their family or friends. Most were probably aware of what had happened earlier in the morning in New York City.

This kind of tragic news would have spread rapidly on those planes, the information secured only from the young.

Probably many passengers were frantically trying to make final calls, or sending voice mails or texts to their loved ones. The passengers knew their earthly lives were evaporating, and they were helpless to stop the terrorists. If you know you are running out of time, then what do you say? What could have ever been more horrible? Each of these dead had been faced with that reality. Meanwhile the terrorists were probably assuring them to remain calm, to cooperate, and they would be returned safely to the airport. Of course, this wasn't so.

One victim was wheeled on the gurney into my small work area. He was wearing a Timex Ironman sports watch, still ticking, and very nearly identical to the one I was wearing. They were only 22 seconds apart. Out loud I wondered why the watch would still be running, and another team member gave me a side hug, and a warm look. Instantly I realized what I had said, but didn't care about the insanity of it. During this time, and in that moment it seemed nothing else in the world mattered, and maybe it never would again. A couple of the team members with me that day recalled very similar experiences, and very specific interactions and conversations with the dead. One remembered talking to a female victim and letting her know everything was going to be Ok. Soon she would return home and be at peace forever.

I'm still not certain whether our personal interactions and conversations with the dead were appropriate. However, it was only natural to respond in a kind manner to those now gone. We did not expect them to respond, but we were up close and personal with each of them. A comforting hand on their shoulder, or a kind word did no harm at all. I personally witnessed many of the staff talking to those in their care, and I knew each gesture was out of deepest love and respect for those now gone forever. Yet, no matter how hard we tried to humanize the situation, it never became easier.

In fact, at times our actions seemed grossly intrusive to those deceased. The dead were so vulnerable and helpless, and our staff only wanted to help. But we couldn't help them. These souls did not arrive with toothaches, and they did not need root canals or extractions to feel better. They were all dead. Amidst this emotional pain and confusion our dental team continued to work courageously. Those early days were defined by dedication, determination, and especially stamina. Following several 16-hour days our team was struggling and tired. We were beat up, and worn down, yet the people on that team maintained their professional demeanor. We continued to press forward, always leaning on each other, and were dedicated to completing the mission. We did what we were asked as quickly and accurately as possible.

The actual working areas were extremely crowded. Inside the small closet-sized examination rooms were not only the two mortuary dental team workers, but the computer, our forensics' instruments on a small table, and the gurney where the dead lie. The workers, and our team, were literally right on top of the deceased. Inside those areas we performed our mission with very poor ventilation, breathing alongside those with no breath, literally decomposing while we worked. Flies swarmed around and seemed to thrive in the environment. It seemed any uncovered areas of our bodies were prime targets, and we had no idea from where the fly had just come.

Our imaginations always assumed the worst. The building was humid, the air was stale and lifeless as the human remains we served. It was an incredibly difficult time, to say the least.

As a group this team was among the hardest workers and the most empathetic human beings I have ever had personal contact with on this planet. Each staff member was endowed with their own individual strengths coming from their own place in life. Each team member was called to this service, determined to do the absolute best that they could. All around us the beat went on. The FBI was fingerprinting remains, AFIP was completing forensic dental exams, and the medical pathologists were prepping for autopsy. This entire scurry around us was within plain view, and the vision was surreal. As if it may not really be happening, but of course it was.

To this day, I am positive each member was at Dover because of a higher purpose. I do believe in choice and free will, but I do not believe coincidence exists in this lifetime. Above all this is a story of faith and hope, singleness of purpose, and deeply inside being determined to serve fellow human beings at any reasonable or unreasonable cost to self. And for those few weeks after 9/11, that is exactly what we did seven days a week. There are no weekends at the mortuary. Tuesday, or Thursday, or Saturday morning rolled around and the team was operating three forensic dental radiology rooms.

We were split into teams, sharing the duties of placing the films into the mouths of the deceased. Outside of the room peering through glass, another partner activated the radiology button. The member placing film wore a lead apron, apparently to protect our vital organs from excess radiation. We also wore lead-lined disposable gloves under our disposable plastic gloves. The lead-lined ones were orange and what I remember most about them is that they were expensive. I have no idea why I remember that, but I do. In fact we would re-use them under the disposable gloves. I remember writing our names on them, and maintaining them throughout the contingency. We were bantering back and forth, trying to keep spirits high, and talking about how tough a situation we were in. We were exhausted, dirty, and feeling extremely sorry for the victims, their families, and to be perfectly honest, ourselves.

Our dental team was located next door to full-body x-ray. Many of those days the full-body radiology team would need assistance moving the deceased onto, or off of the gurney, and onto the radiography equipment. Lifting the remains some-times fell to the dental crew and it was not unusual to see one of our folks lifting the dead from their gurney and helping to hold them into place for the full-body x-ray. It was proximity to the human remains that was the most difficult. Many of the dead had just experienced a plane crash into the Pentagon, and their bodies were mangled, torn, and burnt. Handling these remains so intimately was difficult for our workers. Think of hugging your spouse or child, a warm and breathing human being. This is basically how we were handling the dead weight of those human remains. We hugged and held them close to us while moving them into place. I saw many of the team members with tears in their eyes trying to position an extremity, or move the torso to the left or right. It's hard to imagine, and even more difficult to explain the struggle that we en-countered in those early days in that old mortuary building.

The duty was physically demanding, mentally challenging, and emotionally draining.

As exhausted and emotionally distraught as we were, it was always helpful to remember that many others had gone before. We were not the first mortuary team to deal with this pain, but it was our turn, and we would not let each other, our community, or our nation fail. That old mortuary building had seen many years of these mass casualty disasters including the Jonestown mass suicide. Knowing first-hand what we were exposed to, I just can't imagine in my wildest nightmares what working the Jonestown disaster would have been like. 909 Americans died in that mass suicide in northwestern Ghana, after being misled by Jim Jones and the Peoples Temple. The swish of cyanide would have been their last act, prior to being brought home to Dover and this old building, the same one in which we were now working.

For those three weeks after 9/11 that historic building returned to high glory, as all living and breathing souls inside its ancient bowels were determined to complete accurate identifications on all victims from the Flight 77 disaster, and quickly return the human remains home to those who loved them most. And this we did. Not without struggle, and not without some pain and doubt, but the job did get finished. Our small band of brothers providing dental radiographs was just as integral to the process as anyone else in the building. The effort wound down. The human remains brought to Dover from the Pentagon disaster were processed by the port mortuary in just over three weeks.

For a couple of more months that fall, we were in and out of the mortuary as teeth, or other fragments of the victims would be found in the rubble of the Pentagon. Those small fragments would also be meticulously categorized, identified, and sent to their final resting place. Our duties were fastidious, and the entire staff worked hard to assure that identifications were complete. The toll on our emotions was real, and it was our first challenge of many to come over the next several years. Following the contingency, our team participated in debriefings, and wandered through our lives during the next several months as changed souls. Not only had life been interrupted for us individually due to our exposure to our mortuary duties, but life had changed for the entire country.

The weeks following 9/11 saw many scheduled entertainment events cancelled. Major League Baseball and the National Football League cancelled games, and the Grammies were postponed for a month. Americans were hesitant to congregate in large numbers, especially in close spaces due to the threat of a terrorist event. The concern was very real. Even NASCAR cancelled a stock car race. Ironically the first race held following the 9/11 disaster, occurred at The Monster Mile, a one-mile concrete oval located in Dover, Delaware just a few miles from our military base. My wife and I attended that race which enjoyed every seat full, and was awash in a sea of American flags. A full field of high-horsepower American steel took to the track that bright and sunny day with many fans adorned in patriotically-themed colors of red, white and blue. NASCAR's chosen son, and our favorite driver, Dale Earnhardt, Jr. would go on to win that race, and for those hundred thousand plus fans full of raw emotions, the healing was underway.

For all who had grown up in the land of the free, sheltered by the warmth and love of our country's isolationist safety, the oceans no longer provided a buffer. We were forced to reconcile with the fact that thousands of our fellow Americans going about their routine daily activities were murdered by terrorists. We suddenly were forced to live with the reality that there were people in the world who not only hated us, but were willing to die to kill us. While as military members we were well-versed in this possibility, this was a totally new and foreign concept to the majority of Americans.

Incredibly, our nation's reaction to this tragedy was hopeful and positive. The majority of our country reacted the way a free and proud nation should react. The country pulled together, and we realized that for all of our differences, ultimately we would need one another to survive. We watched on television the heroic actions of New York City's public servants, and a multitude of stories about the generosity of Americans. We wanted to give, and we wanted to share. The popularity of our President soared, and nationalism was at its height for several years.

I suspect there's another perspective of those months and years following for America's Muslim population. There is no arguing that there was backlash against that group, which in many circles extends into today. I wish this was not true, but it is. Though I am no expert on Islam, I have had many practicing friends over the years. It seems to me that individually we are all the same, regardless of religion. The responsibility that we each individually share is to accept the consequences of our actions, and to try to learn from them. Fifteen years post 9/11, I have learned much. I hope you have too.

By late October of 2001, our small team had completed our mortuary duties; and had returned to the dental clinic, to real live patients, and other military duties. Time passed, and we were closer than ever. Reviewing that time, and talking to peers, the months following our 9/11 mortuary contingency were times where traumatic symptoms were escalating, we just didn't recognize them. All were very proud of their participation, and our team had exceeded expectations, along with the entire mortuary staff. Yet, we returned to the clinic with very different emotions than those we had taken into the contingency, and now only had each other to lean on. Those working together inside that mortuary building had become family; loving, caring about and fighting with each other as only those closest to one another ever can.

Who could we tell of our trauma? Rightly or wrongly, there was a quiet understanding among our team, as among many military members that voluntary mental health assistance was out of the question. Maybe today there is better insight, but at that time our distinct perception as active duty military members was that mental health carried stigma. No way would we admit some of the concerns we were having, as all wanted to honorably complete their military careers. Further, most admit there was no way they would have shared any details with their family. We did not want to hurt or traumatize anyone who had not been there. We surely tried to help each other. It was so then, as it is today that sharing with the other team members was the most therapeutic way to rationalize the trauma.

We each understood that something inside us had changed, and there was no going back. There was no way to forget the trauma we had engaged, and there is no doubt it bound us forever through a common and shared experience. So throughout that winter, and for many of the months that followed we worked together to try to get better. Some in healthy ways, and some not, but placed in our situation I fully understand and believe that each of us did the best that we could. My personal reprieve came in orders overseas to Korea. It was a year away from family and friends, but it helped me gain some long-term insight into what I had experienced, and made me realize that I must pursue the road forward.

Soon enough Dover would be reengaged in forensic mortuary preparation and service as America beat her war drums. All knew it was coming, as President Bush stood among the police and firefighting heroes of New York City on top of a pile of World Trade Center rubble and promised that America would respond. Though we did not know when or how that response would occur, at Dover we knew very well that American response may result in casualties. If so, we also realized that those casualties would likely soon be among us. We also knew that the mortuary response and the DERT Team would be ready.

5

THE DERT TEAM

Once in a while in our lives a person or a group of people come along at just the right time. Those are the people that are destined to change everything that we think and believe about the world and our place in it. That is, if we are ready. Be prepared for that opportunity, and don't overlook the very real possibility that the opportunity appears as an impossible task, or work that you are not prepared to do.

The DERT Team story could very well have ended, and been forgotten immediately after the Flight 77 disaster. But it didn't. Just as Daniel Hines had quarterbacked the digital buildup, he now chose to tackle the DERT Team cause. He sensed a higher mission, assumed responsibility for driving the challenge, and marched our little band of brothers and sisters straight ahead. He took the lead on the project of developing a challenge coin specifically for our team. For the uninitiated, the challenge coin is a small military coin bearing an organization's insignia or emblem and carried by the organization's members. Traditionally, they are given to prove membership when challenged and to enhance morale.

Dan is the creator of the original DERT Team coin, the very same one adorning the cover of this book. He went back to the official emblem of dentistry that had been adopted by the American Dental Association (ADA) in 1965. That emblems' origins date back to ancient times and to the god Asclepius, who was one of the earliest gods of health renowned for his healing abilities. The best known of his children include Hygieia, from whose name the word hygiene is derived, and Panaceia from which the word panacea, a cure-all or universal remedy originates. Dan blended this design with the American bald eagle used to symbolize the 436th Eagle Wing at Dover, and a Red Cross to give nod to the 436th Medical Group. On the reverse side of the coin he added the Pentagon logo, with a digital sensor in the middle symbolizing the historical first-ever use of digital radiology in a mass casualty contingency.

The very first DERT coin was issued to our flight commander, for commitment and leadership to her enlisted troops. In very short order the entire team had coins in pocket, as a small token of remembrance for what we had together endured. This small token should never be underestimated, as the coin created camaraderie as a motivator, and gave the team a sense of oneness. We had a concrete, actual memento to bond us, and this idea of the DERT Team was cemented forever. It was a turning point, and certainly enhanced and encouraged our successful service over the following years. Talking to the team over the past year, it soon became clear that identifying a founding member of the DERT Team would be impossible, as it was born in the haze of those cloudy and horrendous weeks following 9/11. However, without Dan's leading efforts in creation of the challenge coin, it seems quite possible that our team would have long since been forgotten.

Further, it would be impossible to say that we had one leader during those years, as each of us was capable and motivated as leaders in our own right. Each team member had a personality of their own, and was willing to defer self-interests for the good of the team. We certainly had informal leaders that needed to step up during our larger contingencies, making decisions and accepting responsibility for the specific forensic duty, but as each team member was self-driven you could always count on every last man, and woman. This team was incredible, whether taking or giving orders. Every single one of them absolutely gave their entire souls to getting this job done. Talking to one of us, was talking to the team, and from the very beginning we all seemed to understand the higher purpose of the incredible situation we found ourselves in. I had arrived on station less than a year earlier, so several of our team members had more experience than I in the mortuary from other incidents. So along with being highly motivated leaders, as a team we possessed the willingness to share experience and knowledge needed to face any challenge. The thought process synergistic and allowed the team to exceed all expectations.

There is not a comprehensive list of all of the members, as the team has always been fluid and informal. Anyone who voluntarily stepped into the mortuary and served alongside our team was considered a part of our humble group. Certainly that number would reach into the many of hundreds. I hope some of them will read this and contact me. I love hearing their stories, and despite the individual trauma suffered, there is a proud brother and sisterhood that go along with this service. What I could share is that we had team members that volunteered from all over the United States military service. Most would arrive into Dover on temporary duty to assist, and stay with us for up to three months. Then they would rotate out, and we would receive another group. Normally the volunteers came in pairs or threes, highly motivated, and ready to serve. We didn't let them down.

Make no mistake; on 9/11 our team had been challenged. On September 11th in the rubble of Flight 77 and the Pentagon, the DERT Team was born. We had served honorably in that old mortuary, and had outperformed all expectations by completing our forensic dental duties full digitally. This was the first time in history, during a mass contingency that the use of a sensor and digital radiography had been practiced. We were proud, and rightly so. Our team had grown very close in a very short period of time, and this experience would serve us well for the horror to come. We had successfully completed our mission in those few short weeks. And ready-or-not over the next several years, and courtesy of the War in Iraq, many of us would have direct contact with thousands more of human remains. Looking back today, we had set ourselves up for success with the nucleus of our team ready and willing to serve in any capacity.

Following those three weeks in the old mortuary we returned to our regular duties in the dental clinic. There were still incidents, and occasionally we would return to the mortuary, but nothing of the magnitude of disaster we'd seen from the Pentagon and Flight 77. It should be noted though; that even going to the mortuary to identify one human remain was stressful, and emotionally complicated. I think this fact would be very easy to overlook in the shadow of 9/11. Every life mattered, and resulted in tragedy for those closest to the victim. Each fallen hero was always treated with dignity, honor, and respect.

Later that year, I received unaccompanied remote-assignment orders to Osan Air Base in the Republic of South Korea, and I was offered a follow-on assignment of my choosing. Although I might not have received my first choice, it was likely I would have gotten one of my top three. For me it was an easy decision. I wanted to return to Dover following the short tour of twelve months, and reunite with my mortuary team. The U.S. Air Force saw it the same way. Many of the team members stayed in place at Dover, and prepared for the opening of the new mortuary building. This included a lot of planning and preparation, and our team was involved in the entire process. Soon all these efforts of building preparation would be tested along with our team. The DERT Team would be ready.

One common thread I discovered talking to the team over the past year was that each of us sensed a deep concern for one another's well-being. We not only liked each other, but understood and cared about one others long-term health.

We thought of each other as family, and this continues to-day. Always sharing a kind word for another is the universal language we speak. In conversations with the team I would encourage an old peer to share their remembrances of their personal specific duties. Invariably, those conversations would end up focused on another team member, and how incredible that other member's service and sacrifice had been. The conversation would always end with a plea to convey in this book the love we felt for one another, and still do.

We were determined to protect each other, and all were quick to volunteer to cover an incident, to save the other from returning to mortuary duty. This team was the exact opposite of selfish, and the true definition of the word selfless. I often hear the Air Force core values mentioned to this day at Memorial Day and Veteran's Day events. All airmen recognize integrity first, service before self, and excellence in all we do as basic core values of their USAF service. We start with integrity first as it remains the bedrock of military service. It's being honest with yourself and others, and always doing what's right, whether or not anyone is aware of your actions. Service members will not compromise the truth, whether in small or large actions. It carries with you throughout your life, and when you take this trait back into the civilian world you soon learn that its practice is invaluable.

The next is military service itself, and the belief down deep in your core that service to this great nation, comes before any personal needs. Military service is a 24/7 commitment of your time, and requires ongoing sacrifice. You've often heard it said, and it's very true that military service is not for everyone.

Today our military remains a voluntary service and the finest fighting force in the documented history of the world. The third core value is excellence in all we do. Military members are entrusted with your freedom, and mine. Historically, freedom has never come easy, and it has never been free. It has required the sacrifice of many great men and women during the history of our nation. For the military member, doing our best is not just our professional duty, but rather has always been a moral obligation.

Looking back I would reiterate my belief that the blend of personalities stationed at Dover following the 9/11 disaster was not coincidental. Regardless of what you or I personally believe, it seems a Higher Power was in control of the situation. This team suffered circumstances of unspeakable horror in completion of duties, but found that together the tasks not only could be completed, but could be completed quickly and accurately. Most on the team were, and are in touch with their Higher Powers, and recognize that relationship as integral to their ongoing recoveries. And when I say recoveries, I specifically refer to coming back to mental and emotional health following this traumatic experience. One of my peer interviews shared a story, and the same script that she shared has played over and over in my mind for years and years. She shared with me that she was drawn to the mortuary almost as if by an unseen force, and she was bound to serve. Regardless of where her regular duties found her, if she was needed, and could get to the mortuary to help, she would be there. The only thing that could keep her away was her physical location. If they didn't want her assistance, they better send her far away.

This was a theme I heard over and over in my conversations with the team. What would we sacrifice to serve? That was never the question. Indeed, each was willing to sacrifice everything, including their mental health and potentially their futures, to return those fallen American heroes home. How incredible are these words and these thoughts? Talking to my teammate from those days, brought tears to my eyes as I fully understood what she was saying, and understood exactly how seriously she meant it. Deep love for other human beings is a higher-calling, and an essential human survival element. When you think about lifetimes and hundreds and thousands of years of humanity, where have we come from? How and why are we here? While the vast majority of human inhabitation of this planet is unknown and undocumented, some elements of our existence appear certain. Human beings are programmed to love, to share and to serve. Observing these feelings first-hand, and being a part of that service was an incredible blessing. For all the suffering, how fortunate we were.

Each of the team has struggled in their own ways over the past fifteen years. Some have made questionable life choices, suffering their own losses, and some have thrived. However, there is no question that our strained emotional well-being has created some familial problems. I often worry especially about our children. What did they learn from their traumatized parents, and how are they today? Children are much more resilient than adults, and hopefully they'll recognize that their parents did the best they could. Several of the team members have suffered a divorce, and though it may be difficult to tie our mortuary service directly to those splits, it's also not hard to connect the dots.

Our service in that building changed each of us; and there is not one doubt in the world, that our loved ones suffered as well. For those that have tried to contain and reason with their trauma, and are motivated to work towards a recovery, I promise you that there is hope. Suffering is a long-term part of the human experience, and many would argue that suffering creates more effective adults. Once we've accepted the pain, and come to terms with the outcomes of the trauma, we have a chance to begin our recovery. The team leaned heavily on each other throughout the pain of their mortuary service, and became very close. Many found this internal team therapy immediately helpful, and this should be recognized.

To this day if I want to talk about my mortuary service, there's only a handful I can call. But, talking to one of my brothers or sisters from those days I know I'm being heard, and I'm thankful to God they have the time to talk to me. Some of us followed up with professional counseling and psychiatric services, and some of us didn't. The reasons for not following up are that we were in denial, and convinced that we could weather the storm alone. The reasons for following up were also simple. We were in flat-out, plain survival mode, suffering post-traumatic stress incidents that we were unable to resolve in our minds, and we were potentially in danger of harming ourselves or others.

We did have available a Chaplain, and an ongoing CISM (Critical Incident Stress Management) Team, led by a mental health professional. These were in the forms of debriefs following our duties in the mortuary, but once 9/11 ended, and the Iraq theatre began, these debriefs became more irregular. Or if they were scheduled, we were too busy to regularly attend them. The work pace became crazy. It wasn't unusual for us to arrive at the mortuary by 6 A.M. and remain fully dressed in scrubs and gowns for 12-14 hours, often for many days at a time. We were functioning in robotic mode. The stress and strain of a never-ending stream of human remains wears on a living soul, and there is no doubt that exposure to these desecrated human remains are a prime indicator for mental health issues.

A common shared thought was that we didn't deserve to be treated. We were just taking up the mental health professional's time and space, obstructing those who really needed the help. After all, we were not the combat soldiers or marines on the battlefields of Iraq. We had not taken up arms, and charged through a foreign city, fighting those who would destroy all that America stands for. Even more incredibly, treatment professionals sometimes would confirm those mistaken beliefs. They questioned how could we be suffering combat fatigue, or post-traumatic stress disorder if we have never set foot on the battlefield? At the time, I was one of those who felt this way, but over time I've changed my mind. I understand now that opening those body bags and facing the blown off limbs, charred remains, and eviscerated corpses of American heroes linked me and my team directly to the battlefield.

There is not one bit of doubt in my mind that the professionals on base wanted to care for our team. The CISM model was just one offering, but we also had access to a wide array of mental health professionals, including a psychiatrist and psychiatric medications for anxiety, depression, trauma or any other mortuary-related malady. Today, team consensus shares the perception that mental health really never helped. Let me be very clear with that statement. It was not the fault of mental health, they certainly tried. Unfortunately, some of us were unwilling participants. Admitting mental health issues is admitting weakness, and threatening our careers. Or so we universally believed. Also, it would be impossible to sit down with the counselor and try to explain what we'd experienced. I spent the final several months of my active duty service in weekly therapy, and I know that the mental health professional did want to help me. I remember sharing gruesome details of a past experience and seeing the professional counselor cringe. Honestly, how couldn't they? If I were in their chair, I'm relatively certain that I'd have had the same reaction. Sometimes it all seemed out-of-body, or a nightmare of epic proportions, like maybe I really didn't experience what I'd remembered. Unfortunately, fifteen years later I realize and accept that it did happen, and our team and I must process those memories to have any chance at recovery.

A Chaplain was always close and helpful with a warm word. Team remembrances of the chaplain's service are very positive. The chaplain was a warm friend and confidant, and someone who you could share your feelings, and yet remain safe. For me personally I felt the same way. My first choice to chat about my thoughts was always a team mate, but the chaplain was a valid and helpful option. They were kind, thoughtful, and always with a larger view of what and where we were. They did not try to save us; rather they tended to lead us in the right direction, and always with a keen insight for the greater mission. They was no doubt that they cared about each one of us. Plus, for me personally I always thought of their connection to the spiritual part of our lives as comforting.

On my retirement day, I was offered Veteran's Administration care, and sent north to the VA hospital in Wilmington, Delaware. A month or so later, I attended my VA retirement appointment, but just couldn't explain what, how or why I was feeling so emotionally sick. Looking back I understand that I was just plain numb. I didn't feel anything, because it was the only way I could wake up and go on with my life. I filled out a questionnaire, and answered questions exactly how I thought they should be answered. Emotional pain strains the memory, and there was no way I would have ever admitted to harmful thoughts. I was certain that I just needed time.

The medical doctor seemed satisfied that I was better, asked me a few related or unrelated questions, and sent me on my way. I was not upset at all and did not want treatment; indeed all I really wanted at that time was to get out of that office and on with my life. My primary interest was in forgetting all about that mortuary, and trying to get a civilian job. I only wanted to feel normal, like I used too. While I had no idea at the time if I could ever feel normal again, I believed I could. I believed I could do it on my own, and that maybe I wasn't that sick at all. Those thoughts were not just my own. Immediately following our military service, many on the team were uninterested in talking about their post-traumatic stress disorders

(PTSD), rather most decided to pursue individual paths in our attempts to recover. We simply wanted to move on.

Our dental mortuary team had arrived to Dover coming from many past personal life and military experiences. We were black and white and brown, country and city kids, and had diverse life experience. We were very different in those ways that do not matter, and exactly alike in all the ways that do matter most. For the military member, team always out-ranks cultural or ethnic difference; just as national interests outranks personal desire. We were all for one and one for all; until the end, and this was a hard and cold fact. We had raised our right hands and sworn to defend this nation with our lives. We swore that we would do anything in our powers to protect your freedom.

My experience has been that military members don't want to be treated better than any other group, but we do deserve respect. The American military are your neighbors and family and friends, and they are offering to sacrifice their lives for your freedom. All military members were civilians first and we understand our civic duties. We had each been to basic military training; learned to march, to accept orders, and to issue orders as necessary. Such a simple premise, it always amazes me that most do not understand that the best leaders are always the best followers. Military time allows for this insight. Military members learn to issue orders, and carry out lawful duties, for the good of a higher purpose. All of this we knew and believed deep in our hearts and souls. There was not one leader on this team; rather this was a team of leaders.

These were incredible servants, and human beings of the highest order, that I was privileged to share a bit of time with on this deep blue planet. When we received our orders to Dover Air Force Base, Delaware we each knew that there was the possibility of mortuary duty, but it certainly was not expected on the scale that we experienced it. While I could write forever about our differences, the lesson was in our similarities. We each believed in a higher calling, and a higher purpose. We lived and breathed service before self, and the opportunity to serve our nation was bred into us at a very young age. We each understood the privilege of wearing our military uniform. We kept our hair neat and trimmed, our uniforms pressed, and our shoes shined. We were not a loud bunch. To the contrary, we were quiet, exuded confidence in a calm and calculated manner, and were consummate professionals. We were proud of our chosen craft, and even more proud to represent the United States of America in the military uniform of the United States Air Force.

Preparing for and experiencing the Iraq war stateside in the Dover mortuary was another time and space. Back then our team was young and just trying to survive in a world of war that none of us ever expected to face. But face it we did, and honorably we accomplished it. Today my friends in Dover advise me that the DERT Team is loosely organized. Just one retired DERT team member does continue to carry on our tradition and serve in the same capacity at the mortuary. Yet, the Dental Clinic itself plays only a minor role in services at the port mortuary. In a way this is very sad to hear, but I do accept it, and know in my heart that if ever called to duty those dental technicians at Dover would again respond. The mortuary duty was a privilege, and an honor. Our team was blessed to arrive together to Dover at the perfect time. Maybe in a way, it was a perfect storm situation, and provided us the opportunity to step into a situation that called for uncommon devotion to a higher calling.

The DERT team accepted our solemn duties, and took them seriously, completing them professionally with dignity, honor and respect. These were steady, dependable professionals, but they shared another softer side. And that was the notion of common courtesy and treating others as you would wish to be treated. The lessons taught and shared from those years were lessons of a lifetime, and I hope all take that message with them. Human beings are good. They mean well. Most people are not inherently evil, though evil certainly exists. The vast majority of the time if you give another person an opportunity to choose, they will do the right thing. This is what I came to believe from all the pain and trauma of my mortuary service. People are good. Following our military service during 9/11, this was the mentality we were taking forward. We would soon need all of this hope for the goodness of human beings leaning forward, as we approached America's military intervention into the Middle East in 2003

6

WAR ARRIVES IN DOVER

Human beings have been in conflict from the beginning of recorded human history. There are no sure answers on why, but certainly heading the list of suspects would be our own individual lack of insight, and lack of sense of purpose. What if we all learned to love ourselves first? Once we were able to control our thoughts and actions, and respect our self, we would be more likely to share empathy for all of those around us. It doesn't seem to me a difficult question. The answer always starts with care of self.The U.S. began its invasion of Iraq on March 20, 2003 joining coalition allies launching a "shock and awe" bombing campaign. American forces quickly swept through the country with overwhelming military might, which led to the collapse of the Ba'athist government. Saddam Hussein retreated into his bunker and was not captured until December 2003. Unfortunately, Saddam's demise created a power vacuum which was filled with widespread sectarian violence between the Shias and Sunnis, leading to ongoing confrontation with allied forces. As for lessons from the Iraqi war, I'll leave that to the experts and scholars. At my level, and my team's level the strategy or philosophy of this war was never our concern. We were dealing with the human cost and the human element. What this meant back home in the United States, was that more American heroes were being killed in action, and returning to Dover Air Force Base in body bags.

For many Americans, including me, this was the first full-blown war of our generation. There had been dozens of military conflicts in the previous two decades. Including Operation Desert Shield launched on August 9, 1990 by President Bush ordering the forward deployment of the U.S. Army into the Persian Gulf region to help defend Saudi Arabia after the August 2 invasion of Kuwait by Iraq. The Allied military buildup continued, led by United States forces and culminating in Iraq's refusal to leave Kuwait. In January of 1991 U.S. and Coalition aircraft attacked Iraqi forces and military targets in Iraq and Kuwait in conjunction with a coalition of allies and under United Nations Security Council resolutions. Then from February 24th to 28th, U.S.-led United Nation forces launched a ground offensive that finally drove Iraqi forces out of Kuwait within 100 hours. Combat operations ended on February 28, 1991, when President Bush declared a ceasefire.

Most my age or younger either could not personally remember Vietnam War, or was too small to remember the conflict. However, many Americans were affected through a family member's service, and were exposed to the stories of

the trauma of those American heroes returning home to a dis-
illusioned homeland. Many of those veterans continue to suffer today. If there are any Americans with a right to be angry,
it would be the Vietnam War veteran. Those veterans from the
Vietnam era returned home to an angry and confused nation.
There is no doubt that those veterans were not treated well
upon their return. Watching documentaries on those years, it
hurts me deeply to see them being tormented and even confronted by the ongoing protests all over the country. The vast
majorities were drafted, and were doing their duty in the service of their free nation. Right or wrong, the war was not the
veteran's choice. Today we should be grateful for, and thank,
the Vietnam veteran at every opportunity.

The 1960's in America were a time of change and confusion for that generation and the nation. I am just old
enough to remember the late sixties; the war, and riots
in American cities being broadcast each evening on the
nightly news. As a child I believed the world was on fire
as Detroit, Baltimore, and Los Angeles each seemed to be
burning down. They were the years of rebellion against in-
stitution, and demands for change and equal rights for all.
They were years that changed America; some believe it was
for the better, and some for the worse. Regardless of where
we stand on the political spectrum one ideal should remain
at the forefront of our thought. Political division and free
speech are not America's weakness, but rather her greatest
strength. Lack of tolerance is the first sign that we are not
practicing democracy. Democracies should always allow
dissent, and encourage different beliefs.

Meanwhile in Dover the 2003 shock and awe campaign in Iraq was the beginning of a wartime era that would change my generation's perception of what we believed war to be. Not only that, but we would soon come face-to-face with the horrors of war, and that exposure would change each of our lives forever. My medical military unit was not combat-hardened; indeed most had only handled a live gas mask during basic training, and our experience with automatic weapons was limited to our annual weapons qualification training. Our entire generation had enjoyed a relative period of peace and prosperity. Active military members were able to live independently on the base with their families, enjoy personal transportation and access to the commissary. Off the base we were treated well, with the majority of Americans being appreciative of our military service. During those years prior to 9/11 we may have complained about annual military contingency exercises and twelve-hour shifts, or remote assignments, but this was all soon to change. Now it was our generations turn to step up, and accept responsibility for our nation's call to service.

Back at the port mortuary our team began to experience a surge in action. Body bags were pouring back to American shores in dozens monthly, and the trauma that is war, flowed back to the land of the free. Of the dozen or so regulars working dental identification at the mortuary during the early Iraqi War years, our experience working in the mortuary was limited. We had experience with forensic identifications in a mass disaster contingency because of the 9/11 tragedy. Otherwise our experience was generally limited to one or two remains at a time, usually a suicide or military plane crash and sometimes spread out over weeks or months. More than half of us remained from those Flight 77 days and created the core of the self-named DERT Team. This experienced core would allow us to complete whatever difficulties that were headed our way.

Soon enough our base and our mortuary team would be inundated with human remains. It was not unusual to receive a dozen or more casualties a day, multiple times per week. Our team began spending more time working in the mortuary, than we did with normal peacetime duties. Imagine the work that we asked this team to perform. In the morning, one of the staff would be radiographing casualties direct from the battlefields of Iraq, and in the afternoon that very same staff member may be taking x-rays on a very alive patient back at the dental clinic. We had few others to talk to about this experience. We certainly could not share our troubles with the live patients. So we continued to lean on each other. This in itself was traumatic and emotionally straining, and only the beginning of what this team would experience over the next several years.

American casualties in Iraq totaled nearly 500 fallen warriors by the end of 2003. I was just returning from a short tour to Osan Air Base, Republic of Korea, and was reunited with my team in Dover by the end of December. While in South Korea I did experience post-traumatic symptoms of my service in the mortuary. Most fortunately I had peers to lean on, to help me through those most difficult times. Overall, my time in Korea was productive, as I was able to travel, reflect on my service at Dover, and explore an entirely different culture. Americans were treated very well in South Korea during my time in that beautiful country. The weekends were often spent in the metropolis of Seoul and exploring ancient temples, climbing mountains, and partaking in some most unusual foods. The mortuary duty break of twelve months in Asia was a good one for me, and I returned feeling determined and ready to return to the mortuary and assist my team.

While I had been gone our team had enjoyed a move into the new, state-of-the-art port mortuary built on the grounds where the old building had been. This was an incredible facility from the bottom to the top. The entrance way revealed a magnificently chiseled stone wall, which was dedicated to the history of mortuary services at Dover, and displayed the contingencies, along with the numbers of human remains identified. The office spaces were modern. The hallways were well-lit, wide and clean. Everything about the new building was exactly everything that the old building wasn't. For our team, the best part was gaining our own space, and enjoying the air exchange system. In the new building, we could breath. It stayed cool in the summer, and warm in the winter. We could wander to our stations without wearing a mask. Rarely would we see a fly. The number one remembrance of my peers who had worked in both the old and new mortuaries, were the vastly improved facilities. I agree one hundred percent.

During this time our team fell into a distinct pattern. Each morning our team would be briefed on the status of the arrival of fallen American heroes returning to Dover. If they had landed overnight, we would be headed directly to the mortuary very early in the morning. If they were in route we would receive a timeline and adjust our schedules accordingly. The deceased heroes would arrive via one of the military transport planes directly from the war theatre, or one of the allied hospitals in Europe. The fallen returned home in metal coffins; inside which were body bags that were zippered, shiny black and moisture proof. The bags were iced down for the long flight to try to impede imminent decay of the deceased human body. The metal coffins contained not only the remains but often the personal effects which would be included in a gallon-sized zip lock bag. Experiencing so many of those lost souls return only deepened the numbness of our feelings. Personalizing the human remains was always problem number one, and a distinct no-no, but often there was simply no way around it. This was personal, especially as many that returned wore the same uniforms that our team pulled on each morning.

Out on the flight line, the U.S. flag-draped metal coffins would be hand-carried off the plane by the Dover honor guards in a dignified transfer. This process is a solemn movement of the fallen heroes from the arriving aircraft into a waiting transport vehicle, which ensures that dignity, honor and respect, are provided to the fallen. Out of respect for the deceased heroes' honorable service, the carry team would be composed of members of the same military service as the fallen. Officially, the dignified transfer is not considered a ceremony, as any undue pressure should never be placed onto the grieving families making them feel obligated to come to Dover. However, the military is fully committed to the care and support of the deceased families, and will assist those families that desire attending the transfer. The military will fund travel back to Dover for the family to the primary next of kin, in addition to two supporting family members.

From the airplane to the mortuary entrance was just a very short ride along the edge of the flight line, and soon the deceased would be lifted out of the transport vehicle, and carried into an elongated and bunkered scanning room. The body bags would be scanned for ordinance or weapons, and if any were found would be safely removed prior to entering the mortuary proper. This room had very thick cement walls, but there were small panes of glass that you could peer into to watch the procession. The small panes of glass were very thick, and apparently blast-proof.

Occasionally I would pass through to visit that area, and hear unofficial stories of ammunition or unexploded ordinances that had inadvertently slipped onto the transport planes while back in the war theatre. These stories were not routine, but also were not rare, as the fallen were often rushed out of the war zone under strained conditions. It always allowed me insight into how courageous those pilots and air crews were. Priority number one for that air crew was getting the aircraft off the ground in Iraq, and back to the land of the free. Those professionals at Dover working with that initial contact of the body bags very carefully handled whatever they encountered. They were munitions experts; well-trained in disposal of any ordinance, and thanks to their high level of competency, and professionalism there was never an explosive incident in that building. At least not that I was ever aware of.

The military is full of ordinary folks doing extraordinary things. And, wartime brings out the best in these heroes. As difficult as our mortuary duty became, one of the team members always stepped up and led. Leadership is critical element number one within any organization, and a good leader is always the difference between success and failure in that organization. Leadership has been defined countless times over human history. In my experience leadership is best exhibited by those with passion in their hearts for doing the right thing, regardless of circumstance. They place their team and their mission ahead of their own self-interests. By taking care of others, they challenge the organization to get better, and ordinarily the staff will respond.

If someone believes in you, and you feel that confidence in your heart, you will do your best to complete your job. You won't require supervision; just solid training, guidance or mentorship, and the opportunity to excel. It's often been suggested in leadership review, that great employees leave their bosses, not their jobs. This I believe to be true. On a military base, that is rarely a problem. Our military leaders were not only dedicated to the mission, but we also knew that they cared deeply about our team. This concern was displayed in many ways, but none more so than when those higher-ranking members would join us tableside in the mortuary. For these souls, I am eternally grateful.

Along with our team, the augmented mortuary workers were primarily volunteers from each of the services, brought into Dover, and rotated into forensic duty. They could have volunteered from any service, and any military station, and generally spent three months working alongside our Dover mortuary team. Many would complete a rotation and return home, soon to volunteer to return to the mortuary. These volunteers were exceptionally compassionate, and dedicated to completing their duties as accurately and quickly as possible.

I had the opportunity to speak to a couple of the augmenters during my interviews over the past year. Without exception, they held treasured memories of their time at the Dover port mortuary, and were genuinely grateful for the opportunity to care for our nations fallen, and to serve their country. Their memories often helped to fill in some memory gaps for me. Maybe because they had a bit more time and space to get clear of the emotional strain and reflect on their experiences. Regardless, they provided valuable assistance, and having them with us in the building provided much needed fresh hands to continue our duties. In Dover, we were thrilled to have them.

Following the body bag scan the human remains would be brought into the main portion of the mortuary building. The remains would be photographed, bar-coded and have identification tags assigned. The mortuary was full of professionals dedicated to details, and for very good reason. In this case, details were critical as it was not unusual to have multiple or even dozens of remains in the mortuary building at the same time. Each fallen hero was treated precisely with love and care, as if in the history of the world, this deceased individual were the most important person ever to live. And they were treated this way routinely, day in and day out.

I promise you that any of those heroes that passed through Dover in our care were treated with the utmost of dignity and respect. Over those years, very few personnel spent more time in that building than me, or several members of our team. All repeat the same message, and have not one negative incident to report. The duty of care for our fallen American heroes is sacred, and it was always treated that way. This sacred work, destined to be completed by the chosen few, and those few never forgot the accuracy and compassion with which their duties must be completed. The team was privileged to serve these heroes, who had sacrificed for their nation. These statements I do not make only in reflection. During our service time in the mortuary we were fully aware of our circumstances, and always grateful for that opportunity.

Our interactions with the dead were frequent, unfortunately bordering on routine. We were obligated to complete dental examinations, often on human remains in complete disarray, and always following rigor mortis. This means the jaw would be clenched shut, and must be opened. Using a wooden vampire stake to pry open the deceased mouth, to allow identification on human remains is an unnatural act. Our team repeated that act uncountable times, mostly with tears in our eyes, and pain in our heart. The job just never got easier, and the emotional and mental trauma would not disappear.

These were American heroes we were serving, and our love for country and our brothers and sisters in uniform absolutely took priority over any and all mental health or substance abuse issues we were facing. It hurts a soul to look into the eyes of those killed on the battlefield. It was an unexpected death. We are talking about 18-25 year olds who feel invincible. Though there's no doubt they understood the very real possibility of being killed in action, certainly the vast majority never believed it would happen.

Until it did; then you see eternal fright under those eyelids, and the death mask of a face knowing their last breath was imminent. What were they thinking? Maybe their thoughts were of their mother or father, or their wife and small son or daughter. So you might say, why open the lids? I promise you we never opened eyelids, but many were frozen open, with eyes staring forever into space, somewhere else in another place and time. They were no longer a part of our world. Our team viewed thousands of those eyes, and it's very easy for me to close my eyes today, in a quiet space, and go immediately back to the pain of those faces.

The process of returning these heroes to their hometowns and families was a specific and distinct act of human kindness. Our team was blessed with this opportunity. We were a hands-on team, and worked diligently within the bounds of humanity and science. The human body begins to decompose immediately after death. Cleaning and disinfection of the body is not only necessary for the mortuary workers safety, but is also needed to improve the mortuary team's ability to accurately complete the forensic identifications. The deceased heroes would be sponged, and bathed, always with special care to remove the grunge of war. I often saw mortuary workers carefully cleaning the fingernails and toenails of the deceased. Hand in hand, caressing the fingertips gently, care being given to each and every detail. The heroes would be wearing full military service dress upon their mortuary departure, including white-starched gloves in the casket. No one would have ever known about a little scrape of dirt stuck under a nail, but still time was taken to meticulously care for each and every fallen hero passing through the port mortuary.

I spoke to one of the workers about this duty, and she assured me that this was the most important job she had performed in her entire life. The hero was placed into her assured care, and she was compelled to do her best. She looked me in the eye, her hand grasped firmly onto my forearm, and I knew she meant it completely when she said, "Every single time." The workers performing this duty never ceased to amaze me. I would always walk through and greet the staff, and they would smile back with tears in their eyes. This was work of the heart, and the work of angels, and those performing this duty were following a calling to greatness. When these dear souls arrived on earth, their mission was prepared. They were destined to serve. I prayed for them by name each morning. There is no doubt in my mind that God was listening.

Following the administrative details, the fallen heroes would have their DNA taken as part of the forensic identification process. A positive DNA identification may be exact, but it takes time to complete in a laboratory. So though our goal was accuracy, timeliness was also critical. We wanted these American heroes returned to their families as quickly as possible. For a quicker positive identification the human remains would be brought into the dental area. Here our team was able to work with ante- mortem radiographs, in comparison to the digital radiographs we were able to complete during the forensic post-mortem examination.

Again details and accuracy were critical, and reviewing our work all these years later I can guarantee that our team was quietly and consummately professional. Accepting whatever manner of destruction the hero's human body had suffered, we always found a way to complete that full set of postmortem radiographs. The destruction of these human remains varied widely, and sometimes just finding the teeth was a task in itself. In interviews with the team, some of their saddest memories were that of searching for the teeth. Often times they would be somewhere else in the human cavity, or maybe outside the body, while remaining in the body bag. And if there, they had to be found, identified, and processed.

Regardless of condition of the deceased, our team was determined and did complete accurate and timely positive identifications. During peer interviews, specific dark memories were recalled of the times we spent digging through human muck or bags of human fragments, memories long-since forgotten by me. I think it was healthy for us to recall some of those hard times, and acknowledge that it really happened. It is important to remember, and good for each of our teammates to hear that not only did it happen, but it was all out of love for our brothers and sisters in uniform. Every living human being that ever was has a destiny, and to deny that fate would be to deny the love that exists in our hearts and the hope that endures in our souls. We are all much more alike than we are different. That realization and acceptance could change our world. Those who served with me in the mortuary understand this prospect intimately.

Following completion of our full set of digital radiographs, a forensic dentist would compare the forensic radiographs with the ante-mortem film. Based on the location of fillings, crowns, or other identifying landmarks inside the mouth the dentist would be able to make the positive identification, and report that this was definitely the correct name and identification. As with all others on the team, the toll on those professionals was immense. Their positive identification was critical. Of course they were highly educated holding terminal degrees in their chosen fields, but they still were human beings completing a very difficult task. Our team looked to them for comfort, and always a steady and kind word. Their stability was good for our team, and their guidance was critical to our success.

When speaking to one of our forensic dentists from those days, he shares very fond memories of the team. He was a civilian with no prior military experience. He reported that prior to coming to the mortuary he was often worried about the state of, and the future of America. He shared that following his experience with our team, his mind was placed at ease. This team, and those active duty workers with whom he came into contact are the best America has to offer, and will always step up to serve. He said that meeting them changed his mind about an entire generation. While civilians may not understand this, I do, and further I understand what a high compliment it was. When I asked if there were any specific memories, he remembers asking one of the team leaders to bring in some extra staff on a Sunday morning. He did not want staff to have to miss church or be away from families. He shared that the team leader he spoke to advised him that "the team was available for whatever duty was needed, for as long as it takes."

Most of America, even those living close by our base in Delaware never understood or realized the extent of the services that their friends and neighbors working in the port mortuary were performing. During those years let there be no doubt that combat did indeed come to Dover AFB, and those in the port mortuary were face-to-face with this tragedy on a daily basis. During those years I never thought of combat in that way, but looking back and talking with others it was true. Exposure to that level of trauma is going to affect most of those involved, regardless of whether they are in the war theatre or not. Each of us that worked in that building understands the direct implications of an IED explosion in close proximity to a human body, or a bullet through the chest cavity or head. We've been up close and personal with it. It is never pretty, and though our culture and our media may glamourize violence, people dying traumatically is not entertaining.

Following the dental examination, the human remains would be brought into full-body radiology before being taken into autopsy and embalming. As we worked very closely with full-body radiology, some of our dental team's best friends were there. It was not unusual for us to push the gurney to their station, and remain for the examination. Seeing the full body radiographs was always very interesting. The staff was professional and very well-educated, and because of their experience understood and could share with us what they were evaluating with the films. We also had the opportunity at times to serve in autopsy as an extra set of hands. The autopsy is the post-mortem medical examination. It is a highly specialized surgical procedure that consists of a thorough examination of a corpse to determine the cause and manner of death and to evaluate any disease or injury that may be present. I have always been inquisitive, and especially interested in science. Standing tableside with the pathologist was always an education, and another chance to serve.

Following the embalming, the final step by the mortuary team would be to service-dress the body, and prepare the deceased for departure back to their families and their final resting place. Working in the mortuary I was able to view the prepared human remains of the fallen heroes prior to their departure and their return home to a final resting place. It was an honor to serve these heroes and as often as possible I was determined to stop by and say a short prayer for these American hero's and their families. The morticians provided final closure for the process. The fallen heroes face would appear natural, resting for eternity. The heroes would be in full service dress of an American military uniform, medals meticulously arranged on their chests, with creased trousers and spit-shined shoes. Soon they would be on their way home.

Our team fully understood that the arrival home of these fallen heroes would create pain for multitudes of family and friends, and that the pain would extend into a lifetime for those closest to these heroes. Each of these brave and honorable Americans had volunteered to serve their nation, many entering service following 9/11. There is no doubt they understood full well that they may encounter the dangers of war. I often hear the talking heads on television speaking of overextended military benefits, and wondering if maybe there is room for budget cuts in the military. After all, we receive a fair salary, medical care, and many other benefits, including access to education. For those uncertain of whether or not these heroes have earned these benefits let me assure you that they have. If you are in disagreement, then please advise me what your freedom is worth?

These benefits should always remain, and those that serve should always be revered for the heroes that they are. I have never met a service-member seeking a handout. The military life is a life of service, and we understand and believe in our hearts that personal actions matter and we accept responsibility for those actions. These incredible young men and women are America's own, our home-grown and beloved forever sons and daughters raised with the deep-held belief that freedom has never been free. The service-member accepts this premise and assumes responsibility for extending this freedom for another generation. I promise you that this generation stepped up, and I am proud of every single one of those who freely choose to serve. These heroes whose story I share were some of the finest young souls that America had to offer, and now with one final stop in Dover, they were gone. We must never forget them.

Who lives on to share this story? It is each of our responsibilities to share our service stories. There is a fair chance that if you were interested enough to pick up this book, that you know one of these families that have lost a son or daughter, a mother or father. And if you don't know one of the fallen heroes, you likely do have family members or friends that have served, or are serving. Hug them every chance you get, because their duty never gets easier. Support them and encourage them, and let them know that you will never forget their sacrifice and love for family and country. Also remember that it is just not the single-serving family member that has sacrificed, indeed it is the entire family.

I am a student of history and have loved reading about civilizations and human conflict since my high school years. Being a native of Pennsylvania, I was especially a fan of the Civil War. My son and I completed the ten-mile march at Gettysburg for his Boy Scout Badge, and as a child I had been on multiple field trips visiting the battlefields and surrounding areas. I understood the premise, and was amazed that over a hundred and fifty years ago, citizen soldiers existed that wanted to change our nation for the better. Not only that, but many of those very soldiers grew up all around where I lived. They were not unlike me, or my family and friends. They had been placed in a situation that demanded service, and they responded. I appreciated those soldiers, and their sacrifice. I had always thought of war as honorable, pitting a higher purpose over individual need. After all, if two opposing sides were able to muster the courage to be willing to die for their convictions, there must be some validity to the impending national actions.

Unfortunately on the ground level, from the individual human perspective this is not the reality of what happens. In the real world, when nations and opposing ideals and cultural beliefs collide, human beings die. Those deaths have affected the history of the world. Who died on the battlefield that could have altered the course of human history with an idea, or a discovery that may have improved all of our lives? Maybe a soldier died at Antietam whose great-grandson would have cured cancer? This has always been so, but is very easy to overlook in the day-to-day lives of our ordinary worlds. However, our team fully understood that during each individual examination we were working on behalf of a family that would be impacted for a lifetime, or a hundred years or more. Many of us have family's members generations or multiple generations past that were lost to war. What would have happened should they have lived?

This is ultimate tragedy of war, and one of the greatest weaknesses of human beings. We suffer continual conflict with one another, and that conflict ultimately seems to serve neither side. There are historical exceptions, for instance the Allied Forces defeating Germany and the Nazis to halt genocide, but there are many other times where the loss of human life is difficult to rationalize. The real question may very well be, will human beings ever rise above our differences, and be able to coexist? Based on our experiences the answer seems to be no, but we have a very short frame of reference. I am always amazed that we humans consider ourselves highly educated, and evolved, yet in a very short moment will resort to violence. Maybe we are not as civilized as we have convinced ourselves that we are?

What if somehow we could maintain a sense of wonder? What if we each understood that our knowledge is limited, and accepted it, rather than trying to convince others of the correctness of our beliefs? What if instead of assuming we understand the world and our view is undoubtedly correct, we took the time to get to know someone much different than us? One of the greatest benefits of military service was my exposure to others with very different beliefs than me, and working with others from very different cultures. Not just within my circle of active service, but also from being exposed to people from all over this giant, incredible planet that we all call home. The greatest strength of the American melting pot should be our diversity, but fostering that strength requires an open, thoughtful and motivated society. Unfortunately, as human beings, we are easily distracted, and generally consumed with self-interest.

To me it seems our nation could benefit from a national draft, just to expose our youths to different cultures, and ways of thinking. We do not brainwash our children on purpose, but a child's experience growing up in the inner city is very different that the child growing up on a farm in the Midwest. Regardless of that background of origin it then becomes natural for us individually to place our own world-view above that of others. It is only natural to assume that those who raised and loved us taught us right. It is probably fair to say that human beings are much more alike than different, but our survival instincts direct us toward exaggerating the differences. Putting young people together in basic military training would certainly be one way to prepare them for our multi-cultural society, and our differences with others all over the world.

To be fair I recognize that there are those with differences of opinion on the military, and those who decline military service based on personal or religious beliefs. I do not believe their position is well-thought out, as without a military, America would not enjoy the freedoms that we do. You might wonder why I feel so certain about this. Think about the vastness of the history of our planet, and our multitude of different cultural beliefs. Human beings have always been conflictual, and there must be some force for freedom, or else evil would thrive. I don't like to think of America as the world's police force. But if we are not, who will help those that cannot help themselves, or are being targeted for abuse and death for their gender, or religious beliefs and convictions. While we cannot save the entire world, we surely can and should save some.

I respect different beliefs, and would allow those who decline military service the opportunity to serve in the Peace Corps, or AmeriCorps, or maybe even a missionary service. Maybe we should force the youth out of their comfort zone and introduce them into a world of service? Even if only for short periods of time, their experience may very well benefit our entire society. My roommate from Yellowstone National Park in the early 1980's went on to serve in the Peace Corps before finishing college and graduate school, and ultimately becoming a Jesuit Priest. While he never served a day of military service, his service to others is exceptional, and he contributed to improving the world, just as our Marines providing food or shelter aid in a third world country is improving the world. Each human being should contribute. If we raised our children this way, with service as a key component, we would live in a very different world.

One of our mortuary team members that joined our team in 2003 was a Marine, coming to Air Force military service following a stint in the United States Marine Corps. He was easy to pick out in our group; highly fit, with the best high and tight haircut on the air base. He was one of our physical fitness leaders in the squadron, and carried out all duties with a smile on his face. We could never be close friends because of separation in our field ranks, but I certainly shared then as now, an affinity for him. We were born in the same state, and he was a quick and dependable running partner. We spent a lot of days pushing each other shoulder to shoulder. Of course, he could never have allowed an aged, pudgy airman to beat him on a daily run. Prior to his departure, he would go on to finish a marathon with me. At that distance, I was a bit more competitive. If you have experienced that distance, you understand the incredible physical accomplishment of finishing the marathon distance. It requires dedication and determination, and this young man had both. He left Dover the same year I had, and had gone on to serve in Korea, before returning stateside.

I had not spoken to him for over ten years, but when he answered the phone I remembered his voice immediately. We were able to chat about his memories of mortuary service. He started with, "I was humbled, and proud. I'm telling you we were silent professionals. We were doing something big, and many on the outside wouldn't realize or understand." Marines always have a way with words, cutting through the mumbo-jumbo of military jargon and just speaking the truth. This young man was accurate in his statement. He recalled his first experience with the mortuary had been a civilian decapitation in Iraq. Holding a human head in your hands is not only alarming, but incredibly frightening. Still he assisted in completing the tasking of this high-profile case. What a terrible introduction to mortuary forensic identification, but with this experience under his belt, this young Marine became a steady contributor to our service, and an important and contributing member of our team.

He shared with me that he remembered the "door-knockers" from Fallujah and the heavy casualties incurred, and how it hurt him deeply. This young man was himself a Marine, and seeing his brothers in arms return in body bags was something he had never expected to experience. For those not familiar with the term he shared that door-knockers are those American warriors going house to house in urban combat, clearing buildings as they move through. There may be a more dangerous occupation in the military, but it's hard to imagine what that may be. When I asked him what he thinks of when he thinks of the mortuary today, he shared "the smell of formaldehyde and Vicks vapor rub, and shoe covers." Yes, I quickly agreed.

Today he has over seventeen years of service, and reports only fleeting emotional concerns from his past mortuary service. Like some of the others he believes he has the trauma compartmentalized in his mind, and feels that he is able to control it. He agrees completely that the trauma remains, as do the quick memories. But he is thankful to seldom experience a nightmare, and thankful to still be actively serving this great nation. This is another of America's finest sons, and our team was incredibly lucky to have him. He agreed that he would follow-up with professional help before his retirement, just to be sure. I agreed that documenting his mortuary service was probably a good idea.

Many of our team members share similar stories of commitment and dedication to their service and to their country. One of those stories stands out, even all these years later. A young airman by the name of Summer Chamberlain arrived to her first military assignment at Dover in 1999 and remained stationed at Dover until June of 2004. She was another key player during those years, frequently volunteering and serving tableside with our team in the mortuary. Near the end of her service time in Dover, I was thankful to see her receive her dream orders and move on as a military recruiter. She shares the story that she wanted to be a recruiter specifically because of her time at the mortuary. She understood that she was in a unique position to share with young recruits the true meaning of humility, patriotism and service. All lessons learned much too well while performing forensics dental identifications with our team.

Summer's story of mortuary service didn't end that June. That year the holidays rolled around, and by early December she had completed recruiter training. She was now a full-time recruiter serving in upstate New York. She had a holiday break coming up, and phoned me directly. She shared that she was going to be visiting friends in Dover for the Christmas holiday, and it would mean a great deal to her to be able to serve again. She was well aware that the team remained heavily tasked, it had been a brutal year, and she wanted to return to the mortuary and help out however she could.

On December 28th the team received word that three human remains were scheduled to arrive in Dover that evening, and would be processed in the mortuary the very next day. December 29th was Summer's 25th birthday, and that same morning I met her in the parking lot of the port mortuary and escorted her back through the solemn hallways of the building. We performed the three forensic dental identifications that morning, and she was tableside with me through the entire procedure. It was very nice to see her again, and feel the love in her heart for our duties. She was able to reflect on her earlier time and coming back I could feel the appreciation and concern she had for those fallen heroes, and their families. We talked about the pain of this duty, and she shared that "We did a damn good job. I don't think that I'll ever heal completely. I have a healthy scar there, but it will never go away." Yes, she summed it up perfectly. These memories are never going away.

She has had an incredible recruiting career for the military. She shared that she wanted to replace all the airmen that America had lost, and was determined to do her best to bring others into the service to help. She says she understands that not all are willing or able to serve, but she wants to help those that are willing. She did so well in her field, that she became a doctor recruiter, ultimately managing the doctor recruiting program at Randolph AFB, Texas. To date, she has recruited over two thousand new airman. She humbly explains that she believes in this generation of young Americans, and that she is sure that freedom will ultimately prevail. On this point, as with many others, Summer and I completely agree.

Talking to her recently she has had even more time to reflect. She sent me a note and shared. "Serving at the mortuary is one of those rare, patriotic, life changing experiences that most will never understand. It's a mixture of emotions – pain, honor, sadness, pride, patriotism, humility, gratitude, anger and hope. We all understood that it was an amazing honor and privilege to return our brothers and sisters in arms home to their families." Our team was full of those who shared these ideals, and beliefs.

The war's arrival in Dover changed many lives, none more so than the members of our dental forensics team. Though we were exceedingly exposed to those very real horrors of war, we have all moved on as best as we could. I am so incredibly proud of this team, and all of those that ever entered the hallowed hallways of the port mortuary to serve. Service is a primary part of being a human being. Being granted this opportunity was an incredible privilege, and being so intimately connected with the fallen was a gift from God. We were completely committed to the fallen and their families. We owed it to those families to return their heroes as quickly as possible. We all were aware of the responsibility of this gift, and never took it for granted.

Those days in the mortuary could very well have destroyed any one of us, but together we overcame the trauma, and excelled under almost impossible conditions. Lessons learned for me from this experience are that there are no winners in war. One side may experience a little less or more pain, but regardless of which side you are on there is going to be a lot of traumatic fallout from the fight. I understand that there will always be conflict between human beings on this planet. I only hope that moving forward our nations' leaders are always conscious of the suffering that will be inflicted, and that they will seek every alternative prior to sending our troops into battle.

7

MY FINAL DAY IN THE PORT MORTUARY

The end of any journey is always difficult. We have spent days, months, or years on the path, and may have even reached our destination. However, once there we quickly realize that we have not reached the summit, but rather the base. And the next challenge awaits us. Always remain aware of your state of progress towards those goals. When it is time to move on, take that step with clarity and purpose.

For me there was a distinct moment in time, and a specific event that effectively ended my service in the mortuary at Dover, and my career in the U.S. Air Force. It started like any other day would have started back in those days. My team had been subjected to thousands of hours of duty in the mortuary, working intimately with thousands of human remains. My team and I had been exposed to the horrors of bodies in all condition of trauma and decay. Our best defense was always to try to stay as busy as possible, and look forward. But that is not long-term reality, and eventually those memories are going to appear at the surface of our very conscious daily lives. I remember so many of the human remains and experiences specifically, but there is one that I will remember until I take my own last breath.

This particular late summer morning had been routine for me. I was awake early, and headed outside for a two-hour run. The base was still quiet. My run started around 4 A.M. so I had the early morning loop around the military flight line all to myself. The sky was clear, and the stars were bright. Out to the east I could see the sky beginning to tint orange and purple, promising another day of precious life on this incredible planet. I was preparing for the Baltimore Marathon in October, and always found great rhythm leading to a deep emotional peace with my runs. Quickly I'd fall into a nine-minute a mile pace and stay there. Pitter-pattering along, slowly but straight ahead. Close running friends have always joked with me that I may be one of the greatest slow-runners that ever lived. I'm not sure whether or not that's meant as a compliment, but I'll take it as so.

Running always provided me ample alone time to think, and to meditate. The time spent running allowed for sorting of problems, considering solutions, and ultimately was a great stress manager. I had completed 84 marathons over the previous fourteen years, and slow long-distance running was one discipline that I had mastered. Though I was never fast, I was always a finisher. And being a finisher at the distance of 26.2 miles makes one a successful runner. That success lends to confidence in all other areas of your life. I'm certain that running is what enabled me to maintain my sanity in the mortuary for as long as I had. Everything in our world must eventually change. Not one of us is immune to trying times, and more challenges. Acceptance of that reality is a part of a healthy life, and my life was about to require complete re-evaluation.

Most mornings I'd begin and end my run at the port mortuary. The new mortuary building was state of the art, including clean, spacious and modern locker rooms for the staff. This morning was cool and comfortable, with little of the humidity of a late August day on the most eastern shore. Running out and away from the mortuary that morning I again felt recharged, breathing in and breathing out. I knew where the dead lay, and that those fallen American heroes would patiently wait for me and the team. Right now I was alive, and I was going to breathe, and I was going to run. My heart pounded as I clicked off the steps, one after another as the minutes turned into miles. I turned at my normal spot at the far end of the flight line and picked up the pace. Off to my right the monster transport planes sit quietly, peering at me suspiciously. The path was narrow, uneven and dark, but I had been out there hundreds of times in all manner of light. I knew each crease in the blacktop, and my steps were sure and straight. The early morning was still, but it seemed I had the wind at my back. My training for Baltimore was right on track.

Soon I was drenched in sweat, endorphins swirling, enjoying a surge of wellness, and back to the mortuary building. I shuffled through the darkened administrative entrance with my badge, and made my way to the locker room, and into the warm and soothing shower. A couple of the team members were already there by the time I arrived for duty at 6 A.M. They were quietly pulling on their scrubs, and gowns, and surgical gear. We had shoes used solely in that building, never to see the light of day. I remember mine well; white leather old-man walkers with Velcro straps, and they were just as comfortable as any expensive running shoe I had ever had on.

Our team had grown very close over the previous four years, and despite the horrors of our duty, we were always able to keep things light among each other in private. Always bantering and prodding each other, and sharing jokes better left unsaid and better yet unremembered. This was probably just a survival mechanism at its most basic. After all, how much death can it be normal to face? Over the previous four years, our exposures to the dark face of untimely deaths had taken its toll on each of us. Anything we could do to reason with the trauma during those years was acceptable. At least it was to us.

The day was lightly scheduled with just one forensic dental examination planned. Our efforts this day would be to work with a case that had not arrived from the war zone. Again I let my boundary down, and listened to the locker room talk. I knew it in my head; under no conditions, do not ever personalize any of the tragic circumstances. Still I reasoned that I had no idea of her specific details, and I would be careful not to notice any of her identifying information. I knew better than to think too much about the deceased, but this time I did, and this time it would come back to haunt me. She had died overseas, and her death was suspicious and being further investigated. When she arrived at our table, she appeared angelic. Her face was perfect. Young and innocent, and much too young to be dead, but she was. This case was a culmination of thousands of deaths over the past four years for me. I'd seen way too many young folks lying motionless, breathless, and cold on this hard, unforgiving, steel table.

We gently kept the young lady covered with a sheet and a blanket. Not for her, but for us. She had to be cold, even I was cold, and I was breathing and dressed warmly head to toe in long underwear, scrubs, and surgical gowns. She was motionless and beautiful all at once, and she lay there as if asleep. Normally while working I was able to disconnect from the reality. I was a professional, and no one in the world was better with those cold steel forensic instruments than me. My motions were fluid, and my work was effortless, and almost unconscious. By this time; like the rest of the core of the team, I was an expert, a master trainer in these mortuary details and duties. Yet, most of the time I checked out mentally and emotionally just in an effort to avoid the pain of the situation we were in.

This time was different. This time I felt directly emotionally connected to this young airman's demise, and my thoughts would not let it go. The questions began to flow, and my brain began to think about the immediate moment. My mind would not stop turning it over. I was in the here and now, and that was a big mistake. Once those feelings started I couldn't stop them. I began to feel very sorry for her and think about her family. I knew in a couple of days, a family member or family friend would reclaim this young body and be faced with the realization that they'd never be able to talk with her again. No more shared laughter, or sitting down for a meal, or talking about the good old days of childhood and growing up. She was just a kid herself, maybe twenty years old, and it was too late. I'd let down my boundary and began to wonder about her world. I knew no specific details of her circumstance or what led her to being here, but I knew she was deceased forever, and there was nothing I could do to change that fact and bring her back. No one could. Everything began to seem so unfair, and my mind continued to grind through the years of pain and suffering that is face-to-face with just one death, only in this case thousands.

Though I had no idea if she had a child or children, I knew she would never see them grow. I knew she would not be returning home the way her family and friends had hoped. Instead, this American hero would be arriving home in full military service dress in a polished wooden casket. Her parents, if they were alive, were already aware of her death and were numb and in denial. Nothing in the world could create more pain than the loss of a beloved child. They probably were notified in the previous 24 hours, and have not been able to stop crying. Or maybe they didn't believe she was really gone. But she was. She was cold as she could be, never to take another breath, and I knew it. I felt it, I felt her family's pain, and I felt all of the pain from those past thousands of war casualties. The pain and reality came all at once, and it was suffocating beyond any hope. This young lady would never know another friend or a spouse, never sit down and enjoy a meal, or watch children gleefully play. I had no idea about anything personally about her, but I felt for her as if she was my own flesh and blood. She had volunteered to serve her country sometime in the past couple of years, and she was going home in a box. It was just all too much, and the moment overwhelmed me.

Fortunately a few seasoned team members were with me in the building on this day for comfort. We did accomplish the full set of dental radiographs, and the positive identification was completed. It was the last dental examination that she'd ever have. Some days our minds wandered way too much for our own good, and this was one of those days. We pushed her gurney on to the full-body x-ray department, and returned to clean and disinfect our own area. Soon our dental treatment room was cleaned, the instruments were disinfected and packaged, and we were done for this day. We all had moments of difficulty during our mortuary work, and sometimes just walking away for a moment or a day was enough. One or both of my team mates recognized I was struggling as the glazed eyes turn into staring and silence. Having them there to comfort me, allowed me get back to the locker room. They tried to talk me through it, and I responded as best I could. Yet the three of us, as well as the team understood that sometimes we just needed space and silence. I convinced them that's what this day called for.

So I sat and stared at my locker until the room had emptied. I thought about the years gone by, and the fallen heroes who were never going home. I thought about all those parents and family members still in pain and quietly suffering. I had helped as much as I was able to, but I could not remain in that mortuary building one more moment. I suddenly realized my time serving in the port mortuary was over. Then I pulled out my old canvas gym bag and emptied the contents of my locker. I had a couple of family pictures taped inside; personal toiletries, two bottles of Gatorade, and a couple of energy bars. The old-man, white leather shoes and my old combination lock found their way into the garbage can. I slam-dunked them with tears in my eyes. Then I walked down that long bright corridor and out the front entrance one last time. The promising day had turned cool, overcast and dreary. Rain was coming. More than four years had passed since Flight 77 struck the Pentagon, and my service in the Port Mortuary was over.

Thinking back on that day always sets my mind back in motion, and reminds me of the deep sadness that continues to exist in my soul. The loss of any life is always a tragedy, and is met with pain from those nearest the deceased. Though I did not know this young lady from Eve, she had touched my heart. I will never personally meet her family, but to me they are my own family. God Bless their souls forever.

Often times I hear friends of my generation talking about young people, and their lack of willingness to accept responsibility. This is probably true with an element of the population, but has not been my experience. During my years in the military I was surrounded by those young folks who had decided to serve their nation. Raising their right hand, and swearing to God, to put their families, freedom and country ahead of themselves. Those that voluntarily put on our nation's military uniform and serve are incredible human beings, and in this nation of ours they have always existed. In times of trial, they will step up and always do the right thing. This is an integral part of what has made America the greatest nation on earth. We are free people, and determined to further that freedom to our children.

Reading stories about our nations' wars, especially the Civil War that divided this country, it's not unusual to read of a sixteen-year old in battle. Indeed, these youth are why America enjoys the freedoms that we do today. However, our current generation touched me a bit more, as they were all volunteers, and they were all working with me. I knew them first-hand. They were and are my family and friends. Any one of them could have been home playing video games, taking classes in college, or working an entry-level job, but they weren't. They were serving their nation. Is this not an honorable undertaking? Are these not honorable human beings, and heroes?

That is how I had come to see young Americans during those final years of service. I knew there was trouble in the world, and those who didn't feel committed to military service, or even some who protested military service. On the other hand I knew full well there were many young and dedicated Americans who were intensely committed to that service. That young lady, lying cold and still on my steel table was one of them, and another of her generation's greatest heroes, another of America's finest. I did not pursue her personal story immediately after leaving the mortuary, but I did see her in the news and was aware of her name, and her plight. I never wrote her name or details down, but her memory always resided in my heart.

Months later on national media I heard another mention of her as the investigation into her death continued. I followed up and learned the details, and those details further broke my heart. She had grown up near my hometown. In the course of a human life, what could cause one to want to harm another? What stressors or circumstances would be worthy of ending the life of another human soul? In wartime, regardless of whether I believe in the cause or not, I do understand. Human beings are bound to survival, and when they feel threatened will take up arms. But why would anyone want to harm another for interpersonal reasons? Why not just walk away? There's no way to explain the corrupt actions of the human animal, but I must concede that evil does exist in this world.

Acceptance of evil in the world has not corrupted my thought with negativity, but it has made me more aware of how, where, and with who I spend my time. I try to place myself in situations to succeed, and to serve others at every opportunity. When I am able to serve, it not only helps those around me, but ultimately helps me. Learning to care for self has been critical to my recovery, and though I have not mastered that service, I am on the path. Happiness and satisfaction is not static, yet cannot be pursued. Those feelings have always been inside me, as they are inside you. When we are positive with our intentions and actions for others, those feelings and actions always come directly back to us.

This ideal has been a critical component on my road back to full productivity in society. All along the path there have been challenges, and opportunities to improve. Sometimes I recognized them, and sometimes I did not. Regardless of this, I feel like I ended up exactly where I belonged, and doing what I was meant to do. My advice to my old friends on the team is to continue on your path with an open and hopeful mind. Our experiences have molded us. Though my final day in that mortuary seemed to destroy any chance I had at recovery, in the long run and fifteen years past I fully realize that specific day only strengthened my life and my faith. For this opportunity I remain grateful.

During my interviews with my peers over the past year, the team offered few recollections as specific as mine in their final days of mortuary service, but their feelings about the years gone by are eerily similar. One of the staff shared with me her recollections of her final couple of years at Dover, many years after I was gone. She reported that as many of the core group of the DERT team departed, there were fewer staff stepping up to help. The dental clinic became less engaged with the mortuary, and the team had less and less people to help. She felt the pressure was on her to perform, and she had to get the job done. No matter what she could not fail or let her team down. She shared, "I think it's because we saw so much trauma, and you know how hard we were all working, and trying to get these remains back to their families. If I didn't do it, who was going to do it? There was so much pressure. You had to be on call for the weekend, so I was on duty every weekend, holidays, and all the time. And I would feel bad if I could not go to the mortuary. Just the thought of saying no made me feel guilty, because I was so committed to it." She spoke quickly, but I heard and documented every single word. I was so sorry to hear this pain in her voice, and understood exactly how she must have felt. I only wish I could have been there to help her.

She shared that when she received orders to a new assignment away from Dover, she was well aware entering the mortuary that final time, that she most likely would never return. She told me she took in the surroundings with tears in her eyes, and held her humble service to those American heroes as among the greatest experience of her life. Walking the halls of the mortuary would be a foreign, maybe a frightening experience to most, but for those of us who had served many years in that building we understood the immense honor within those walls. She shared that good and bad memories flooded back to her, and especially thoughts of how that team had become family to her. She asked me to share that "above all our team cared for and loved one another, not only based on our shared horrific experiences, but because those staff were indeed very special servants, every single last one."

She reported that completion of her final identification was without incident, stressful and sad as usual, and that when she left she said goodbye to that American hero, and that building. She reported that it was with mixed feelings that she departed, and that she felt connected deeply in her soul to her service there. Just like me her feelings were that the only way she could ever really leave that building was to be physically separated from it. If she had remained in the state of Delaware, anywhere in proximity, she would always be drawn back. If the team asked for help, she would be there, she had to be there. She said "it was as if that mortuary duty had gotten inside her, and became a part of her identity, and there was no way to separate herself from it." I was on the phone with her, but her voice was intense and honest, and touched me. I knew what she was saying was honest, because my feelings were exactly the same. To this day, if there were a large contingency, and I had any way of getting to the port mortuary, or being allowed back into that building, I would demand entrance, and quickly serve again.

While talking we both understood what we were saying was honest and true, but just the same we both understand we could never return. Fortunately, we're both a thousand miles away from Dover Air Force Base, and will never be asked to help again. This is our saving grace. We are grateful for what that time and service meant to our lives, but we understand that it had to be over. The time had come to move on with our lives, and moving on would be difficult at best. Indeed, for me that is what this book is all about, and I believe in my heart it will offer the same opportunity to our mortuary team. She still loves that team as do I, and we both want the same thing. We want the others who walked away from the port mortuary after that final identification, to find peace in their hearts. It is a difficult journey; but there is no alternative to navigating the path, it is the journey that each of us must take.

8

THE PAIN OF PTSD

There is a decades-old conflict over the etiology discussion in professional mental health circles regarding the diagnosis of post-traumatic stress disorder. My concern has never been with the genesis of the symptoms. For me the bottom line is, do we believe the afflicted or don't we? My thoughts are to meet the individual where they are, and if that person is stuck in an emotional quagmire, attempt to build a therapeutic relationship with them, and help move them along.

The term post-traumatic stress disorder was introduced in the early 1970's following large incidences of military trauma immediately following the Vietnam War. In 1980, it was officially recognized by the American Psychiatric Association (APA) in the third edition of the Diagnostic and Statistical Manual of Mental Disorders (DSM-III). There is no doubt that PTSD existed much earlier, since the beginning of human conflict, and from the beginning of warring tribes inflicting trauma to their adversaries. Trauma has been more practically recognized and documented since the 17th century and during the World Wars was described as war neurosis, combat fatigue, or shell shock.

PTSD is a mental illness that can develop after a person is exposed to trauma. PTSD is thought to be triggered by a traumatic event, and comes with a cluster of signs and symptoms. These may include the persistent recall of the event, emotional numbness, and avoidance of feelings or thoughts that are connected to the trauma. Others may suffer from hyper-arousal, find it difficult to concentrate, or have a very difficult time sitting within a small crowded space. There is a long list of risk factors to developing PTSD including; military combat, seeing people die, handling human remains, and exposure to uncontrolled or unpredictable stress. The military officially estimates that around 15% of all combat service members have full-blown PTSD. There are no estimates for those of us whose duties included mortuary service, and have been exposed to thousands of human remains. My best unofficial guess is that among traumatized service members that I personally know, that number would rise well above the official estimate.

Our team's experience with mortuary work, and exposure to human remains certainly predisposed each of our team members to vast amounts of trauma, just as it exposed those on the combat battlefield to trauma. The primary difference being that bodies arrived at the mortuary deceased, whereas those in combat often experience the horror of death first-hand, often times being close to those who were traumatically killed. This is not to compare military combat with our mortuary experience. There must be an inherent fear of directly facing those, who given the opportunity would destroy you. Of being placed in a situation where you kill or be killed. I cannot imagine the horror of the soul's internal battle, when faced with that dilemma.

Looking back now my mind is much clearer, and the picture of our team's encounter with PTSD is much more focused. As will be described, during those years we were frazzled, and confused. For me personally, professionals did their best to help me, I just wasn't the best patient. In fact, I was often a bad patient. For the mortuary team during those years, we may have recognized that PTSD was a problem, but often didn't take the time to properly deal with it. Our excuse then, as now, is we were very busy, and we were. Looking back there were signs that team members were having issues that needed addressed. Some were making poor personal choices in dealing with the pain we were suffering. Personal and professional relationships struggled as each of us were facing our own internal pain, and trying to disconnect from the active demons of our daily realities. Alcohol is legal during military service if you are over 21 years of age, and is a potent drug that allows one to temporarily disconnect from any horrid reality. Emotions often overflowed, including anger and high anxiety, and spilled into our daily activities. Others completely checked out, including me. I was living much of those years on auto-pilot.

Talking to my team today, there were multiple team members who voluntarily shortened their military careers as a result of their mortuary experiences. From the outside, and even during those years, many around us were not properly processing the experience, reasoning that if our brothers and sisters were dying on the battlefields of Iraq, how in the world could we complain about our personal emotional struggles? It seemed apples and oranges, and I personally believed that flawed theory for a long-time myself. Now I know better, and understand that exposure to human remains in those numbers, by the thousands, are not natural regardless of the circumstances of those exposures, and most certainly those exposures had to affect the mental health of all of those involved.

After a while the doom and gloom of the escalating trauma appearing in the mortuary started to seem normal, with our reactions to the daily horror muting our senses, and numbing any and all of the feelings we were able to have. After all, how sick or emotionally disconnected did we need to be to get a mental health diagnosis? Or even more interesting, why would any of us have wanted one? From our perspective as active duty military members we believed whole-hearted the following. A mental health diagnosis while on active duty was terminal. You were done, no more promotions, and on your way off of active duty, and off of the base. Also, rightly or wrongly, there was a commonly accepted thought that if diagnosed, they would take away your personal firearms. Some of the team were active wild-game hunters, had grown up with shotguns and rifles in the home, and the thought of losing those kept many away from much needed mental health care. As pointed out earlier, in the fog of the trauma, we were unable to always make the appropriate decisions regarding our own care.

Immediately after leaving the mortuary I was a walking, living and breathing zombie, and those months between leaving the mortuary and leaving the military were strained emotional times. My family and friends, were aware enough of my altered and bewildered state to direct me to the mental health building. I was in denial and was certain that even though I was struggling, with time, I would recover. But weeks turned into months, and I was not getting better. Fortunately for me friends at work intervened. With the advice of a dear friend, I took myself to the mental health building. I agreed as I understood my military career was near closure. I had adequate and honorable time served for military retirement, and now if I needed help, felt hopeful to acquire it.

I was familiar with mental health as our team had sat through many, many critical incident stress management debriefings in small team groups in the same building. Some seemed to find the groups helpful, but I wasn't one of them. As earlier disclosed, I was a bad patient. I was certain that if I admitted what I was thinking, feeling or dreaming about I'd be locked in a padded room, and shuffled immediately off of active duty with a looney discharge as described above. I was not sleeping through the night. Often I would wake up sweating and thinking about the fate of that poor soldier I'd just seen pulled out of a body bag, or even worse having a full-blown nightmare of another day in the mortuary.

Anyone who has ever suffered from traumatic dreams understands the tragedy of a never-ending nightmare. If you can't go to sleep to forget, then what is the alternative? I never seriously considered harming myself, or anyone else, but I certainly gained a better understanding of those who do. I understand the idea of giving up the hope that things can get better. I've reasoned with trauma, and considered options, and somehow I have always managed to find someone to talk to or something inspirational to read, or to listen to, that pulled me out of the darkness. That does not mean that I ever expect them to disappear. At this point, all of these years later, they have become much less intense, and an accepted part of my life. They are very infrequent, and though frightening, my unconscious response to them seems to be lessening. The mind is amazing, as within moments of sleep, you can be transported back in time for years and years. Today I am thankful for a better understanding of my personal situation, and have accepted the fact that there are many past circumstances in my life that can never be changed. However ten years ago, my ability to cope with them was much different.

The dreams were frequent, traumatic, and realistic in those early days after leaving the mortuary. Several times a week, and always involving direct-care on human remains. The dreams would routinely vary in specific details, but the theme seemed generally the same. Though I'd left the mortuary behind in the real day-time world, it seemed the mortuary's grip on my soul, and my unconscious mind held tight. Slipping off to sleep would fine me working diligently in the mortuary, alongside that cold steel table once again, with those sharp, stainless and gleaming tools of despair. The cold stainless steel was lifelessness in personification, and even today when I pick up any kind of knife I feel it again. I'm back inside that building, and always take just a moment to say a small prayer. In my dreams, I held the deceased in my hands again, without gloves or gowns and faced those mangled and lifeless bodies.

Other staff wandered in my dreams, around the building in the low light, and I could always hear their rumblings of discontent. In these dreams, it was as if my co-workers were themselves deceased, only taking a break from death, to torment my thoughts. I was certain I could never finish my tasking. I stared down long lines of body bags, occasionally stopping to unzip one, and find a friend or family member peering at me from inside the bag. The smell of death and formaldehyde was always there in my sleep, as the smell is with me today. On one of these anxious nights I was working alongside one of my mortuary dream buddies. We were working on completing a full set of digital radiographs, and couldn't hold the gurney or the body still. It seemed to be wobbling in danger of falling over at any time. No matter what we did we could not keep the skull in position for the shot. Finally my partner grabbed the head with both hands in a tight grip allowing me to place the digital sensor. Suddenly, the top of the skull exploded off, and the brains of this pour soul spilled onto the floor.

Sometimes my unconscious had me wandering the hallways of that vast horrific building. I could see one of my peers coming towards me smiling, and waving as if they were thrilled to see me. They would be carrying a bag, and though I knew damn well what was in that bag, I would smile at them and wave back. They came closer and closer, and I was comforted seeing a familiar face amidst the cold and grey of the buildings steel lined corridors. They would always warmly greet me, and hand me the bag. Their response was always that the deceased were ready. They were heroes, and wanted to go home. I'd open and peer into the bag and find a decapitated human head. I wouldn't scream, I'd greet the poor soul, and head directly for my table. I would take the head out of the bag, lay it gently on the table and begin the process. Another one of my teammates would be there with that vicious vampire stick. We would pry the jaw open, and peer directly into the oral cavity.

There were often maggots inside, feasting on the remains. I would calmly scoop them out of the way of the film, and continue my duty. Soon the examination would be complete. Now this soul could peacefully be on their way home to family and friends. The horror of these dreams remained so vivid that I could remember the details so well once I was back awake. I would sit straight up in my bed, in a cold sweat and crying, immediately heading into the bathroom to hide. Laying there curled up and sweating, I often wondered about those poor families that had sent a loved one to war, only to have their head returned. What pain they must live with, a deep pain that could never be healed. I prayed that the families would never know, but deep inside I realized that they would. After all, any of us would be interested in how our loved ones passed. I wandered around aimlessly, and easily frightened during those early days with the heaviest of casualties. It seemed that those days would go on forever. We were well beyond shell-shocked and only functioning out of love for our country, love for each other, and our determination to serve those who could no longer serve themselves. The team had leaned on each other for a long time, and that had to be enough. No one else seemed able to help us; we were going to have to save each other. So that is exactly what we tried to do.

Not thinking about the horrible experience seemed to be another common survival mechanism, but sooner or later you have to go to sleep, in the dark. Being next to someone in that bed, who loves you forever, is comforting, but they can't really save you from yourself or those memories. In fact, most of the team haven't told their partners the extent of the details, and have hidden the trauma in the best way that they could. Looking back, the reasons for our confused state was simple. Our beliefs were flawed, but at the time, they were our real beliefs. Why share the trauma, who does it really serve? Further, how does anyone share the experience of this trauma? If in our experience the professionals looked at us in disbelief, what chance does your untrained family have?   Fortunately for me and most of the team, time has tempered our thoughts. We now generally understand that these are experiences that must be personally confronted and shared with someone willing to help us.

Once my mortuary service was complete I did seek treatment. During my very first mental health appointment, the psychiatrist immediately found me agitated and depressed, and prescribed me medications to help me sleep. I probably should have listened to the doctor, but being hazy from the trauma, I refused them. No way would I submit to ingesting chemicals to improve my mood, as I felt in my heart that the best mood enhancer in the world was exercise. I had used running for years to stabilize disposition, and it had worked wonderfully. Its simple science, exercise makes you tired. But there was no arguing with the mental health professionals as they were determined to attempt to help me, so I began picking up my prescriptions as directed. I never swallowed one though. The psychiatrist ran me through a series of tests, and evaluations and within a couple of sessions he determined I did indeed have symptoms of trauma. I not only believed and understood his interpretation, but I was certain that it was true. I didn't need or want any diagnosis; I needed to know how to get better, or more accurately I needed to know how to forget the horrors I had seen.

So for several months I went to see the mental health counselor; with the psychiatrist stepping in occasionally to proclaim that my psychiatric medications were working wonderfully, and my mood and my mental health was improving. I never lied to the mental health professionals on base, I just didn't respond to what they didn't ask. That is, I didn't offer information. And to be fair, I was improving. Separation from the mortuary building was indeed most helpful. Even though my world was spinning, and I was often lost in spirit and soul, I reasoned that if I could fool the doctor, maybe I wasn't so sick after all. Now I know that it was not the doctor who ultimately helped me, it was the counselor who believed me and listened to what I had to say.

I never saw the counselors' notes and did not care what he wrote. I liked and respected him. He always seemed to hear me, smiled when he could and nodded a hundred times an hour. He looked me in the eye when I talked. When I cried, he shared empathy and warmth, and let me know that he heard me, and that it was healthy to share those feelings. Though he hadn't been with me, our team, or the dead at that cold steel tableside, he did seem to care. And that mattered a lot. When he looked at me, I knew he believed me. This trust allowed me to open up a bit more, and talk about some of the specific instances that were seared into my memory. It's not natural to experience a human body in all matter of splatter; having been squished, dismembered, or burnt, but experiencing these things with thousands of human bodies is unnatural beyond description.

Some days I could see it in the counselors face. I was disturbing him with my revelations, with experiences that the team and I dealt with routinely on a daily basis. He would be speechless, with his mouth almost trembling, staring at me, with me staring back. I was the patient, so I'd sit and wait for him. If I accidentally smiled out of nervousness, it would really freak him out. And to be fair, I am not certain how coherent my shared memories were. Sometimes he would open up one of his big, fat books in order to formulate a response. His mouth would open and he would mumble some official serious sounding terminology flying directly over my head. Honestly, if I hadn't experienced the horror, it would have been difficult for me to process my own recollection as reality.

This counselor really listened to me, and that was enough. This counselor should receive credit for improving my life situation. He couldn't save me from the pain and confusion, but he did throw me a lifeline, and he certainly did the absolute best he could based on his own experiences. I continued to see him during my final several months on active duty. However, once I was officially retired he released me from counseling. At that point he provided me with a referral to the veteran's administration. It was hard for me to understand how he could release me because it seemed he was helping. I wasn't interested in driving an hour to a weekly appointment, and I was certain in my heart that most mental health professionals had no idea what our team was facing in the mortuary. Further, it was not going to be me to inform them. Once through the pain of that memory was enough, and I was not going back.

It was not the counselor's fault that I did not follow-up with his recommendation; there was just no way for me to start over, and to fully explain to another mental health professional that our team was exposed to combat on a daily basis … for years. Talking to my team over the past year has been enlightening, and has allowed some healing, hopefully for us all. Some have followed up with care and have been diagnosed, and some have continued the battle alone. This is where we are, and trying to find a way forward is just part of the journey. While a few remain on active duty, they are nearing military retirement, and mostly understand the need to consider the status of their mental health. Insight has improved for us all, but insight has not necessarily meant action.

Triggers remain for the majority; driving down the road and observing dead animals, or the smells of barbeque restaurants. Following my retirement, I still haven't returned to a Burger King restaurant, because of the odor. I prefer not to grill meat over an open flame, if at all possible. From time to time, I will decide maybe I am better now and should try it. But the memories are still vivid. The smells of charred human beings following a burning plane crash are very distinct, and not a smell that could ever be forgotten. If you can close your eyes and imagine the smell of your favorite food, then you understand what I am saying. That smell is always there, just like those horrific smells that we experienced.

One of the team members described being followed by a hearse every time he tried to drive somewhere. He reported that it seemed each week during errands he would look into his rearview mirror and see one of those big, old black Cadillac's following him. Soon he had begun to quit driving, only going out as needed. But sooner or later he would have to travel somewhere. So while driving he would stay on the lookout, and wait patiently at corners to assure the coast was clear for him to make a run for milk or bread. He shared that his greatest fear was that the hearse was coming for him or one of his family or friends. Further, he said I was the only person he had ever told this too, because he knew I would believe him. We agreed that most could never understand.

The fear of death is a natural fear, and experienced by a large part of the human population. When death becomes such a routine part of your world as our mortuary experience allowed, it would seem that fear of death should disappear. And for some it did, but for a few it seems they experienced the opposite effect. Especially while we are young it is easy to feel as if we will live forever, and that we are strong and invincible. Our culture and the media lead us on in this way, glamourizing and encouraging dangerous and risky behaviors. For those who served in the mortuary, that world view was turned upside down. There is nothing funny or entertaining about multiple gunshot wounds to the torso, or an explosion that dismembers a human body.

The primary age-group we saw deceased were young, strong military members in the prime of their lives. While there were many remains that were horrifically disfigured or bloated from water, there were many others with a single bullet-hole wound, or nary a wound at all. Those were the difficult ones, who such a short time ago, were just like any one of us, and lying on our table appeared asleep. Often times they would be wearing the very same uniform we had changed out of in the locker room earlier that morning. Nametags were the worst. Even if our team made a conscious effort to avoid the ongoing war news, it was impossible to avoid some of the larger stories. Watching the national news tell the story of a recently killed American hero was difficult, but then having that soul on our cold steel table made it even worse.

The team members I have talked to agree that there is life after PTSD. Most of the team has faced and accepted the horror of our immense trauma to some extent, and with time most have been able to continue to be productive and satisfied with their lives. So while it is very easy for me to remember back to specific instances, and ongoing occasional dreams, I have found hope among the living. Small matters really are small matters. Everything in my life is about stepping back, and thinking of the more important pieces of our existence. That does not mean I ignore the details. To the contrary, the small moments in life are what make it worthwhile. Don't get me wrong. I am not the know-all, end-all expert on trauma and I am not pretending to be. If you are battling PTSD I understand that your experience is not mine.

My suggestion to the team or anyone suffering from PTSD is to please tell someone, and follow-up with professional help immediately. Educate yourself as much as possible regarding symptoms and strategies to combat them. Ultimately, the power will be yours, but you have to be emotionally healthy enough to accept that power. Gaining insight into the illness, and accepting those experiences that cannot be changed are early steps. Coping mechanisms vary widely, but my thoughts would be that if it works for you, and does not harm yourself or others, use it. There can be no waiting for validation of the care; you are the one who will finally save yourself. This is what I heard from my teammates over the past year, and has ultimately brought some joy into my heart. The team is hopeful.

This is the reality of post-traumatic stress disorder. It is not something that goes away; and though there are treatments, for me long-term care would better be defined as harm-reduction. Some days are going to be better than others. You will experience times when the darkness is overwhelming, and you are sure that life is over. Believe me, it isn't. The key factor in getting better is by not giving up. Use whatever means helps, so long as it is not harming others. I am not sure why the team member's were each affected by this trauma, and recovered or did not, in such different ways. What I am sure of is that it is possible for every single one of us to successfully move on with our lives.

The trauma of those years will never leave, as the memories are etched into the recesses of our human minds that are untouched and unthought-of by science and modern medicine. For me the only possible way to remove the pain of my traumatic mortuary experiences would be to remove my memory. And, who would ever want to do that? After all, even with all of the pain, there was much joy and love, and lessons learned. There is no denying that all of the team members are very different souls following our mortuary experiences. Further, I have not talked to one member that would trade that time for any other military assignment. In fact, the immediate team members that I've interviewed define their time in Dover as the best assignment of their military careers. I feel the same.

Post-traumatic stress disorder is very real, and remains a serious threat to the wellness of our team, and indeed to military members all over the world. While our team is in various stages of returning to pre-mortuary wellness, the majority is functioning effectively, and has gained some sense of relief. Maybe the truth is that we can never return to those earlier days of innocence. As I disclosed early in the manuscript, for me personally life will always be divided into pre and post 9/11. This is not good or bad, it just is. And though my struggle has been tremendous, and at time debilitating, I would not trade a single moment of that time. It made me, as well as the team, who we are today. Someone had to be called for that service, and our team is unanimously in agreement that we are grateful it was us who were called.

9

AIR FORCE RETIREMENT

Time on active duty service will end for all career military members. Some stay longer and some shorter, but many will cling to that strict mindset of personal behaviors long after the uniform has been taken off. What else would you expect? Any action that has been repeated faithfully for over twenty years of your life will be a habit that is difficult to break. Give yourself permission to be whom and what you were meant to be. You served honorably, now it is time to move on.

Looking back today I have a much better understanding of some of my actions during my transition to civilian life. I was only trying to get better. I wasn't ready to retire, though I had completed twenty-one years of honorable service and I was eligible for military retirement. Rather, I retired because I was unable to face another day in that mortuary, and I was unwilling to move to another station to close out my military career. At retirement time I was disappointed in myself for not being able to continue working in the port mortuary to help my team. Now I realize that I departed the military in survival mode. I retired just after a couple of other close friends closed their military service, and others would follow my path in the following years. We couldn't stay in the mortuary forever; we'd served our time, performed honorably and now we had to learn to move into the next stage of our lives.

Change is seldom easy, and moving on from military retirement is difficult. New challenges awaited us, and for the retirees among us, we had not had a civilian job in over twenty years. I remember thinking many times over those final few years of service that if these tragic years in Dover ever ended , and we were able to walk away healthy I would be thankful for as long as I live on this planet. The reality did not meet those expectations. Even though I had spent the final several months in the care of a mental health professional, and was not back in that mortuary building, it was very hard to stay away. I would drive by the building each day. Some days my car would pull into the parking lot by itself. It took all the strength I had to not set foot in that parking lot. I behaved like an addict who needed to return, and that leaving my team was a dereliction of duty on the highest order. There was no getting around it, and now I fully recognize that many of us experienced it in the exact same way. I liken it to stories I hear of exhausted combat soldiers or Marines vowing to return to their units in Iraq or Afghanistan. They fully understand that they are returning to hell on earth, but they must be with their brothers and sisters in arms, to live or die. Breaking that thought process was difficult, but anyone engaged with and then departing those circumstances must face it. None of us are larger than the mission. The mission will go on, and other Americans will follow in our steps, just as we followed in those before us.

My retirement ceremony was held at the Air Mobility Command Museum adjacent to Dover Air Force Base. There was not a large crowd; but most of our mortuary team was there, along with my family and some friends. I was grateful that my wife and son; father, mother and sister were able to attend. I know they were all very proud of my service, as I was very proud of each of them. The ceremony was dignified and worthy of a long and honorable military career. I stood at attention near the podium as my commander read the retirement order releasing me from active duty. I felt outside myself, humbled and honored, and looking around at the faces of those present could feel the love and care they had for me. Not just from my family, but from those who had served with me on this terminal military assignment at Dover. There were twenty-one years passed, and countless other military friends, but there was no denying that this was a special group, and I was a part of their family. Together we had worked, shared, and accomplished something much greater than ourselves that would last forever. Even during that immediate time I fully understood that this assignment at Dover had been special, and I knew that all on our team were bonded for a lifetime. There is no other way to put it; each of those serving was destined to be there, and each of us to some extent depended on the others to save ourselves.

The mortuary relationships were not something that we explicitly talked about during those years, whether performing our regular military duties, or performing our war-time mortuary duties. In many ways we were our own little outcast gang, with our own idiosyncrasies and our own structure. That is we shared a structure within an already highly structured military unit. It was unspoken, and unwritten, but it was just as real as these words that I am writing. There were difficult times, and conflict within our group as each had their own ideas about the *who, what, when and where* questions that routinely arose. Just as quickly as the conflict came, the dispute would soon disappear, and we would return to our stable familial military unit. Our experience reminded me of the old television show M*A*S*H; in an episode where shenanigans were ongoing, until the chopper arrived. Then it was business time, and all quickly became serious. There was not one leader, we were all incredibly strong leaders, and that strength created a bond that sealed our lives together. It was us against the world, and we needed one another desperately. We inherently trusted one another out of necessity. The environment that we were placed in to perform our duties was terribly unnatural at best, and in worst case scenario, way too difficult to talk about with the uninitiated. We spent many days crying together. We laughed together, often times very inappropriately maybe to the point of sacrilege. Yet, in those difficult times that nervous laughter was our only defense, our only ability to remain stable and sane.

We did not expect others outside our group to understand, and this premise was understood by all of those who had personally experienced that morbid circle of mortuary service. This team that had shared the past four mortuary years with me had become my family, and they remain so today. I know it is true because during interviews with over ten years passed, I heard it in their voices, some of whom I had not spoken too since leaving the military. No matter, ten years later, we understood the joy of sharing with one another all these years later. I suspect that whether it was ten years, or a hundred years the feelings would have been the same. Love when it is real is forever, and has no concern for the passing of time. Feeling that love is joyful beyond measure, and the feelings during that retirement ceremony were feelings of love. I knew it, and the team knew it. As stated, some had left a year prior, and some would remain a bit longer, but life for all of us had changed forever.

Just over a year after my military retirement ceremony I would lose my father, and the trauma of my mortuary service would again be reignited. I had no way to know it or understand why, but I did understand the intense pain that came with the news. It was unavoidable, and broke my heart. I had been out of the military for a year, and away from the mortuary for well over a year, yet the grief of that mortuary service was just below the skin of my emotional surface. The news sent me into a tailspin, and I cannot offer an answer for what helped me through those years other than God, and the love of family. Fortunately I have a wonderful extended family, which closed ranks, and cared for one another. My mother and sister were always available to talk, and no matter how crazy I behaved my wife and son continued to support me. Love of family is a great blessing, and if you have that, you have a chance in this lifetime. My advice to youth is always to be thankful for the time you had or have together. Those years sure pass by much too quickly.

The death of either of our parents is a trauma of the highest order and in itself will force you to reassess your entire world circumstance. It forces you to accept your mortality, and though I had spent years facing death daily, losing a father is not an event you can prepare for. But prepared or not, it happens to all of us, if we were lucky enough to have a relationship with our father to start with. I had a wonderful father and family man. He loved us all, was proud of us, and made sure that we knew it. He had served in the military with the U.S. Army during the Korean War years. He served just one enlistment. I am sure he was happy to return home to his family, friends, and civilian world. He didn't speak of his service often, but growing up I had seen pictures of him in uniform with his buddies, and remember seeing his old Army uniforms hanging in the basement.

Mostly in his own military pictures my father was smiling. I always wondered why, but now all these years later I know exactly why. Military kinship is among the greatest relationship forces in life, and those fortunate enough to have experienced that closeness are blessed. My father never influenced me in one way or another to join the military, but I knew at a very young age that it was something that I wanted to do. My enlistment probably surprised my parents as much as anyone else, but I had always known and felt bound to serve. Never did I imagine I would spend so many years on active duty, but

I do not regret one moment of it. Rather I am thankful for the friends and experiences shared, and the lessons learned.

My mom remains the most supportive of all my relationships on this planet. I often hear people say, or write on social media that they have the best mothers in the world. They are wrong. I have always had the best mother in the world. Regardless of where I was going or what I was doing, she always believed in me. She not only would say it, but I could always feel it in my heart. This is maybe the greatest asset any human being could ever have, a loving mother. She always deferred her own best interests or needs for her children. In my early adult years, she'd always have a word of support, and made sure I had gas to get home, or to get wherever I was headed. To this day she loves my sister and me more than life, and was married fifty years to our father, prior to his death. She remains resilient and determined to share love in this world. She continues to provide a great example to those around her; out walking daily, and always with a kind word for those around her.

I wasn't sure what I was going to do following my military retirement, but I knew I had to stay as busy as possible, and as soon as possible. My military time had been used wisely. One of enlistments greatest benefits is the promise of a college education. But it is you who has to act. I had earned not only a bachelor's degree, but a graduate degree in counseling. This allowed me to quickly secure a full-time job in the community. Those early days as a civilian worker were difficult. I had gone from active duty in direct support of my beloved country, to working in the community as a counselor. It was difficult to reconcile my feelings, but ultimately the ability to continue service in some capacity was enough. Soon I was integrated into the civilian team, and working with those most mentally ill, with severe psychologically debilitating mental illnesses. All those years looking death in the eye, turned into sitting in an office and learning perspectives on life from a schizophrenic. Perspective is always fruitful and the opportunity to learn never escaped me.

I was thankful for a full-time job in my community, and in those early years I gained invaluable insight and education into severe mental illness and addiction. The resident psychiatrist was a natural and thoughtful mentor and teacher. Along with the social services program manager together they felt that performing weekly counseling sessions with one of our most delusional patients would somehow be good for me. At the time I wasn't appreciative, because of the massive frustration of a schizophrenic patient, but looking back I was placed in the absolutely correct situation. Still numb from my military service working directly with schizophrenia allowed me to gain a better understanding into my own often limited insight into my own well-being. No matter how much I personally hurt emotionally, I still was able to reason, and when awake to respond to those internal demons. It would take years to gain a foothold on my stability, and to move forward, but I never lost hope, or desire to get better. I was always thankful for opportunity, and life itself.

My influences during that time turned from young service members and military peers to civilians. Those were civilians who had spent lifetimes serving their communities, by working with drug addicts and the mentally ill. When I say drug addict I don't refer only to opiate or cannabis addiction, I also refer to alcoholics. Some seem surprised to learn that not only Is alcohol a potent drug, but quite possibly the most effective depressant ever created by humankind. Learning this was a turning point for my thought process. I became intimately familiar with the teachings of Father Martin. I was an immediate disciple and beloved convert. I gained hope, gained focus, and could recite Chalk Talk by heart. It had been stunning to accept, but after years of battling my own depression, I accepted that I was personally responsible for much of my own mental illness. When I greatly reduced my alcohol intake, my mood suddenly became much better. Maybe I knew all along I was doing incredible damage to my physical self and my relationships, but maybe I just didn't want to get better. Maybe avoiding the pain and the trauma I'd suffered was easier than dealing directly with it. At this point, looking addicts in the eye, I knew I had to get more honest with myself to enjoy any sort of productive life.

With this knowledge gained, I'd become much more interested in addict behavior, finding it much more predictable and familiar than mental illness. It took me a couple of more years to understand, and believe that addiction truly is a brain disease. The years following my retirement were a battle for understanding my own self-harming behaviors. As if treading water, I never felt doomed to drown, but getting out of the pool did not seem possible. Alcohol was a quick escape, the easy way out, and when in enough pain the addict will reach for his medicine. There is no excuse in my words, as I now understand the measure and depth of the traumatic experience of mortuary service. I have forgiven myself, and this manuscript is meant as a final, forgive the pun, death blow to the pain of who and what I was all those years ago. There is no doubt that my actions hurt some of those closest to me, including family and friends. I have done my best to make amends, and to move forward. Some have forgiven me, and some have not. I understand and accept the response. Now I understand in my heart that every single one of us is doing the absolute best that we can. Sometimes a human being's best just isn't very good. Yet, life must go on.

One of my first civilian professional peers was an old substance abuse counselor with thirty-three years clean of alcohol. Graduate degrees may be important in the treatment of addiction, but if you want to be really honest, then experience to go with that education is invaluable. His education of me picked up where the professors and books left off. He shared his history with me, and much of his behavior mirrored my own. We were soon not only peers, but close friends. He shared with me a long history of impulsive actions, depression and anti-social behaviors. His early life had been marked with anxiety, low self-esteem and a lack of confidence. These feelings blurred his relationships and made it difficult to participate in daily life. He shared with me the early blackouts, legal problems, and broken relationships. It was a story of suffering, but also an incredible story of redemption. By his mid-twenties he was homeless and alone, and his description allowed me to understand the concept of rock bottom. At this point he'd entered a twelve-step program and was reborn to life. He gave credit to his Higher Power, and explained to me that addicts need to find something outside of themselves, something greater than their selves, to ultimately save themselves. This is a good lesson for all of us to learn, and this gentleman came along at a very critical point in my life.

Along with my counseling education, he provided some color outside the lines, sharing key points of a counseling education that are often over-looked in graduate school. He taught me about real personal responsibility, and although I had enjoyed a lifetime of self-reliance and relative success, it was fantastic to re-hear it at the stage of my life where I needed it most. At this point, just a couple of year's post-military I knew I was destined to work with the addict. I may not be able to save any of them, but I figured there was a good chance I may be able to save myself.

Eight years later I hold terminal credentials at the state, national, and international levels as a substance abuse professional. I'm the first to admit that they're only letters after your name, and will not save you. You must save yourself. Yet I'm very proud of the self-growth in my life. Today in the sunshine of Florida I continue to seek knowledge. One thing I've learned in my lifetime of education is that the more I've discovered, the more I've realized how very little I know. As I continue to write out my thoughts and feelings in this exposed journey, it occurs to me that my transition to civilian life is nearly complete. That military person that I was will always be a major part of what I am, but there is hope and joy in the future. Maybe someday I will even enjoy being a civilian.

What I would share with those still serving in uniform is that a beautiful world waits on the other side of the door of active military service. You will miss some things about that service, most notably the close bonds of friendship you've built and nurtured, and a very common mission. What you will not miss is those early mornings when on an exercise contingency. If you were overseas, you won't miss that personal relationship with your weapon, chemical gear and gas mask. Sure they were good times, but humans generally remember experiences better than they were. After all, it was very difficult to enjoy a bright, sunny day in full MOPP gear, especially when the weather was warm.

You'll never go through that experience again, but you will treasure the memory. You will be sentimental at times, and when standing for the national anthem, or crossing your heart, or bowing your head in prayers you'll probably feel a tear creeping in, then rolling down your cheeks. You'll quickly try to wipe it away, but always remember you earned every single one of those tears. You know first-hand the sacrifice made for our freedom. The knowledge that you helped to sustain America's freedom is a treasure greater than could ever be bestowed on any other living soul. It's incredible looking back, but when we raised our right hand and swore to defend liberty and freedom, we were notably serving ourselves as well.

Freedom is at the essence of what being human means. Human beings were not meant to be caged or detained. Human beings were meant to be free to choose, and with military service all service-members play a critical role in guaranteeing that world for every American, and indeed the modern western society. Being a civilian is not without its own challenges, but your military career has prepared you well, and once you cross over the hardest part will be letting go of that past. Just like others that came before you, you will succeed. Working with civilians is not difficult. Some are committed and some are not, but all are moving forward on their own paths. Some will admire your service, maybe even be interested in what you've done, and where you've been. So you'll hang some of the old military plaques on the wall, and once in a while think about those days.

I have a beautiful plaque from the mortuary, but reserve it for a room in our home. It has a portrait of a painting of the Charles C. Carson Port Mortuary prominently displayed alongside my name, and the years I served in the mortuary. There is also a poem engraved by Robert Herrick and first penned in 1647. "Gather ye rosebuds, while ye may, Olde time is still a flying, and, this same flower, that smiles today, tomorrow will be dying." Nearly four hundred years ago, it was written to remind young women of their fleeting beauty, but today it certainly is appropriate as a remembrance of my mortuary service. I pass by, and read it each day, and think back about the good times and bad. We've all experienced each, and if we are lucky, we will arrive at a place in our thoughts that we realize that those remembrances are most often of our choosing. Choose to remember the good, but never forget the troubles. After all, life is only as good as we make it.

10

TODAY IN FLORIDA

Living in Florida is not unlike living anywhere else in the United States with few exceptions. The primary difference being the relatively mild weather, even in the deepest of winter time. I can take the heat, but no longer do I tolerate well the cold and snow. My belief has always been that the ever-present and sometimes stifling heat may affect human behavior in unusual ways, though I have no way to prove it. No matter to me, I'll take my chances and continue to enjoy the sunshine.

Following our mortuary experience, I often wonder and worry about the wellness of the DERT Team. How are they doing today? I've spoken to all those closest to me during those mortuary years, and I've found a common thread and support. The answer may very well be within each of us, but a professional mental health worker is probably not going to coax it out. We have each accepted responsibility for our own recoveries, though each was quick to concede that a helping hand is always welcome. We find solace in one another, just as those who've gone to battle find comfort with their brothers from the battlefield. Though I haven't maintained contact with my team as well as I should have over the past fifteen years, this lack of contact is going to change moving forward. I keep all of the teams' phone numbers at hand, and if I'm feeling down, I know one of them will be available to talk to me, and to share my struggle. They will certainly do the same. We are no longer alone with our mortuary pain.

Together we are dealing with the continuity of our feelings. The pains of those years are categorized, and we have each accepted how we have been affected. Yet, leaving the mortuary duty was also traumatizing, because we knew exactly what our departure meant for all those still serving. The mortuary would still be open, and always will be. So our departure meant that others would be forced to face the very same traumatic exposure that we did. Military members will continue to decease, and mortuary workers will always be needed to serve, but our time was over.

Opening up to others while in a traumatized emotional state takes a plan. Only those who you trust the most can be allowed into the circle of pain. After all, no one wants to be labeled or considered damaged in any way. Military members are supposed to be strong, and tough, in many ways immune to pain. Though I now realize that was flawed thinking, I can share that paranoia is common among those exposed to such trauma. In those early days, I pulled away from family and friends, and began to slowly fade from the day to day responsibilities of reality. Acceptance of my suffering has helped, and time has been a very good friend. Moving back to Florida was further helpful, but the mortuary building's physical proximity to me was only a small part of the problem. I hope this manuscript is another step forward on my journey of leaving the pain of the mortuary in our past, where it belongs.

It has not been easy for me to write about some of the most traumatic aspects of our experiences. Writing of the horrors of our exposures to human remains is not meant to demean, or disrespect our American heroes in any way. I pray that is not how this manuscript was received by the reader. Unfortunately, war does indeed produce these circumstances, and denying or hiding the aftermath would be dishonoring all those involved. I only pray that we have each learned from this experience. This book should be reviewed as a symbol of hope, and a tribute to all that is right and good about America. Further, it should be a testament and documentation of the human spirit, and the human beings resolve to serve. Our team cared for others, and we treated others as we would have wanted to be treated. Those fallen heroes' of war who passed through our teams' lives can never be forgotten. They were our brothers and sisters who will forever be in our hearts.

Are their exceptions to empathetic human behavior? Yes, in the course of human interaction there will always be those less concerned for the welfare of others, and those that are less motivated toward the opportunity to serve. Let them be. Stay away from the negativity. Let the poor soul choose their path; let them move in their own way. Your time is not theirs. For you, find the light; follow your path and maintain your faith, and find another and another who are where you want to be. I promise there are many out there just like you, and just like me, determined to serve so long as we ever live on this planet. Life is beautiful my friends, there can be no doubt of that. We have opportunities in this free land that have never existed in the course of recorded human history. Let's not let that opportunity go to waste. Enjoy each day, share a kind word, and smile at others every chance you have. The vast majority will quickly return the smile.

Throughout this writing experience my thoughts have been redirected to my own circumstances and my own fate. Those years among the dead were very difficult to come through, and with this book I'm making a conscious effort to end that journey. I am determined to gift myself freedom for tomorrow, and to maintain continuous hope in the human condition. Probably over the past decade much of my emotional problems have been self-inflicted. I have chosen who and what to listen to, and who and what to avoid. I have not always chosen wisely. At times I lost faith in myself, and considered myself to far down the lost path to ever turn around. This is not the right way of thinking. Each of my peers from those days suffered their own personal journey. Not only that, but there is no doubt that 9/11 affected many others much more brutally than it did me or others on our team. For each of those souls lost in the World Trade Center, the Pentagon, one of those doomed aircraft, or the Iraq War, there are many dozens of family members still suffering.

All of these years later, it is up to each of us individually to find a way forward with our lives. There are no correct answers, and logic is not always the rational choice. Human beings are above all, heart and soul, and caring for those pieces of our being is what allows us to remain stuck where we are, or to grow. Some have made the successful transition, and others will follow, but I know for sure that each of us will find a way out of the darkness of those years. Each of us has a dream to create a better world for ourselves and our families. Though that dream is shared with humanity, ultimately our path is ours alone. This is yet another valuable lesson I learned from the pain of working among the dead.

Conversations with the mortuary staff resulted in much shared agreement on the road forward. Such as, no one can take your journey and your greatness away from you, so don't worry in that way. When you are ready, your dream will be there waiting with open arms. It's not an easy road, and there are no shortcuts. You have to be honest with yourself, look in that mirror, and do the right thing. You have to do it over and over. If it's not your time, don't worry, it will be. There is goodness and greatness awaiting each of us. This may seem like trivial self-talk, but for those in recovery, these reminders are essential. Regardless of the trauma we experienced, all agreed that ultimately we each survived with our dignity intact, and are much stronger for the experience.

The writing and sharing of this manuscript is another step in the path forward for our team. I realized many years ago, even during my mortuary service that our experiences and actions should be documented, and I was determined to make that happen. In the early years after my service I tried, but I was still emotionally lost and in pain. I just could not keep the words and thoughts flowing. It just wasn't time for it to be written, but I continued to document thoughts and notes as the years passed by. A year ago, when I sat down to organize notes and to write, I could feel the difference in my own soul. I was beginning to feel emotionally healed well enough to share. Not completely healed, but consistently progressing along the spectrum of wellness. Today, I continue to get better, as does the team. Time may not heal all wounds, but it has certainly improved our emotional health.

Options for improving our emotional, physical and mental health are abundant in today's society. We have unlimited and ongoing access to others through social media contacts leading to individual supports. Today I could have a conversation with a friend in Texas, or Europe, or in Korea. The world is ours. Further, I have found the military community to extend well beyond my years on active duty. Though I have been retired from the Air Force for ten years, I still self-identify as military, and expect that I always will. On a recent weekend, I was sitting with my wife for breakfast at a Cracker Barrel in Daytona Beach, when an active-duty U.S. Army soldier and his wife sat down next to us. He was easy to spot; physically fit with close-cropped hair. Standing erect and with an easy smile. He recognized an old military hat I was wearing, and was quick to approach me with an open hand, a hug, and a thank you. I've found this to be the rule rather than the exception; the overwhelming majority of Americans, and especially those fellow veterans, appreciate our military service.

This unspoken bond of service is a strong one for all former military members, and has been very helpful in my ongoing recovery. It seems the help is always better between individuals, than at the organizational level. I often hear complaints from friends, and in the media, about the Veteran's Administration. These complaints are so frequent that it's hard to not believe that some of them must be true. I do not deny this, and understand that serious problems most likely do exist. Personally, those have not been my experiences, and I recognize and fully accept that I have not been fully served by the V.A. because I haven't allowed myself that service. God knows they have tried.

Though my picture on it is awful, I carry my V.A. card proudly, and always enjoy visiting the facilities. Mostly I enjoy the contact with fellow veterans. Talking to others with a shared perspective and common life experience is always valuable. Should I come across a military brother or sister in need of care, I will always go out of my way to help. My advice is to walk directly into one of the V.A. local centers, or hospitals, and to make sure the center has your information. I also try to offer ongoing contact if the service member needs help. While I may not have an answer, I surely will help them track it down. I hope my brothers and sisters in arms will practice the same, help one another when you can.

If it is you who are still suffering, remember to always surround yourself with those who want to get healthier. You do have a choice. You must get better, and you must refuse to continue to suffer. Beware the negativity we are bombarded with in our media. Start with a single positive soul, and hang on.

Share your dream, and build a circle. There are support groups. Or you may find those seekers such as yourself at church, or if military, seek out a local Team Red, White, and Blue (Team RWB) group. They are best described as a Veteran's of Foreign Wars (VFW) or an American Legion without the alcohol or cigarettes. Team RWB is group of veterans, and friends of veterans, committed to improving the lives of those with whom they welcome into their circle. Their common threads are service, fellowship, and exercise.

Getting better is a personal responsibility and you are, as am I, quite capable of making that transition back into wellness. Do not allow others to dictate your circumstances, this is your life, and you have the power to respond. Remember that you alone are the star of your existence, and you have the power to make it a good life, full of hope, joy and love. Improving your world is also encouraging others. What kind of society do we want to leave to our children? Should our free-will, almost unlimited personal freedoms, and multi-cultural society not be considered a great blessing? Why do we allow outside forces and negative influences to drag us into the pain and confusion of the struggle? We spend so much time looking for the flaws in others, that we neglect that person in the mirror. We need more love, and each of us is capable of sharing that love with others and continuing to grow.

Individually, it would be wise to respect diversity for the strength it brings to our society, and not tolerate any circumstances disavowing that reality. I'm speaking not only of diversity of race or religion, but diversity of thought and speech. Always grant others the freedom you desire. Encourage it joyfully, and as it will certainly be returned to you. If unable to tolerate an individual action or belief, then walk away quickly if you must, but do not allow others to trample the love that fills your soul. Encourage others, and always remember that you and I, and all others were chosen for greatness. Life is a miracle, and our time is now.

Today I'm living in the Orlando area, working full-time in community social service, and have been accepted into Doctoral School at Southeastern University of Florida. My classes start in July. My best defense from my mortuary trauma over the years has consistently been to remain as busy as possible, and surround myself with the lives of hopeful and positive people. Working in community service is a good place to find these souls, and though the work is often frustrating as some of our clients seem to continually make poor life choices, I am able to continue to offer others personal choices. One of my civilian friends here is quick to remind me that we change others' lives by our example, not by our opinions. That is, do not try to tell others what to do, but rather show them what to do through your actions. This is very good advice for all.

Most of my peer professional contacts here in this area have no idea of the extent of my trauma from those years past, and most could never understand. I do not expect them too. That would not be fair. Rather, I leave the past alone in those circles. While interviewing the team I found this to be the rule, rather than the exception. Some of our team members continue to hold much of those years inside, as if cocooned from the world. We don't want or need empathy from family, friends, or peers anyway, but what we do need is some sense of normalcy. We need the opportunity to go to work and continue to serve, to see the joy in others when they're performing that same service. Maybe that's what we all need, and maybe that's enough to help us through difficult times.

For me, along with my faith, family, and work, baseball has been the most consistent extracurricular joy of my life. It was a part of my childhood, and a part of my world that has never changed. There are still nine players, and nine innings. There is no running out of time. You must complete all twenty-seven outs. If there is a tie, then you play on, but still there is no set limit on the time it may take to determine the winner. Maybe that's the comfort of my chosen sport, with all the change in the world, baseball is the one place where I know the rules, and the rules haven't changed. Then there are the baseball cards, which will easily transport me back to a time and place of youth and innocence. I still remember riding my banana-seated bicycle down to the corner store to buy them. At ten cents a pack, I would arrive as an eight-year old shiny eyed kid. The grumpy, but kind, old proprietor would turn over ten packs to me, never charging me the few cents of tax. I studied the teams and had favorite players. Back then, just like today, my love of that sport remains.

Today, here in Central Florida, I follow the Tampa Bay Rays, and my wife and I have become big fans over the past several seasons. Not because they have a long history or tradition, they were just founded in 1998, but because they are a part of something larger that has been around and stable for a century and a half. We each have our own way to disconnect and find comfort, a guilty pleasure if you will. Baseball is my safe way to do this. You can imagine my delight when in the second half of the 2015 season the Rays announced that all veterans would receive free admission to every game following the All-Star break. I made myself a permanent fixture at their stadium, enjoyed the camaraderie of their fans, and the spirit of the history of the game.

For the past fifteen years I've been chasing a sense of normality. Or, I should say, trying to feel like I did before the trauma of the mortuary. Now I know that was never meant to be. That young man that followed Ed Anderson into the mortuary immediately after 9/11 was completely different than the broken man that walked out of the mortuary in the fall of 2005. Now I realize, it is not that I am better or worse, but I am certainly very different. Early in my pursuit of recovery I chased outside sources, and made my own poor choices. Until 2010, I was physically still too close to that mortuary building. It may be hard for others to imagine, but just knowing that it was only three miles from my house was difficult. After all, what if they called me to come back? No way would I be able to refuse. I'd have immediately returned and would have fallen further down that emotional hole. That hole is dark and deep, and climbing out has been the greatest challenge of my life. All the symptoms of PTSD are real, and team members who confided in me all those years ago, and again over the past year in interviews deserve to be treated for their trauma. I highly encourage them to pursue and accept that treatment.

For me the years since have been a blur. Physically, I was defeated. I gained weight, lost energy, and was unable to pull myself out of my own state of disease. There were moments of hope; times when I thought maybe I was again becoming myself. That pre-9/11 self, but it never happened. Throughout my active duty service I ran daily. This was very therapeutic in managing those emotions during difficult times through those final years in the mortuary. Outside I was free, and in the fresh air I was able to maintain sanity. Once I began to gain weight, and stopped running it was a slippery slope. Just a few pounds make a big difference, and off active duty I didn't have the peer support to keep moving. So I slowed, and continued to gain weight. It was a vicious cycle, and soon I found myself unable to run. So I walked. Especially back in Florida the warm weather became easier to enjoy. I was back outside and moving, but still stuffing the emotional pain, and overeating. The recovery is ongoing and I fully understand that I'll be facing this struggle for the remainder of my life.

Today, I am not healed, but I am so much better, regaining my old self-mastery and motivation. I find myself smiling more, and feeling hopeful. I still carry too much weight, but I am outside walking regularly, and breathing in fresh air. It is that old twelve-step adage, one day at a time, or for me, one step at a time, and it is true. Getting serious about documenting this journey was an important corner for me to turn. This book may not be the answer to all my prayers, but it is certainly is a continuation of the path forward. This work has put me back in touch with those friends that suffered with me. Hearing about their journey, helps me with mine. Each day I'll continue to get up, face the day with a smile, and pursue my goals. The team reports the same. Each of the team members that I interviewed for this book has healed to some extent. They too are on their own path forward, and are hopeful that tomorrow will be a little bit better than today. Finally, and most importantly, each of my old mortuary friends realize that the duty they performed was honorable, and each of us are very proud of the duty we performed.

At this point in my life I have come to re-think this entire mortuary experience with a different mindset, accepting that my immediate proximity to this large-scale death experience was a wise teacher. I've decided to accept the pain, as it was. This experience was much bigger than the pain. This was an opportunity to make a difference in our world. Yes, 9/11 changed everything in our lives, but to survive we must choose not to stay in that misery. I choose to think of the positive force that we shared with our world. Working with the human remains of America's fallen heroes was a very sacred and chosen duty. Our work was directed by a much higher force than ourselves, or those around us. That same positive energy is now available to each of us on the journey forward. I'm completely fine with whether you believe, or don't believe in a Higher Power, but for me there is no doubt at all.

And after all is said and done, it seems the key to each of our journeys is the acceptance of our folly. Currently in America, we live in a society and culture that seems determined to separate us, not only from each other, but from what we need deeply in our hearts. Is media driven technology really our friend? For some, technology has rendered them bulletproof. Some are certain of their genius, and unable to accept the imperfect knowledge each of us shares. This is a dangerous way to live a life, but that world is very common. I see it daily.

Each day I make an effort to connect with a stranger while out on my daily routine. Not to meet and share with them personally, but just to look them in the eye and offer a kind greeting. At times, this is not easy to accomplish, especially with the younger crowd. The vast majority are lost in their electronic world, choosing virtual relationships over the warmth of friendship. I often wonder about those virtual friendships, and how they will affect the current generation over their lifespan. Time will tell. I am not placing judgment on this choice, but it does make me wonder about the depth of human needs.

Surely many thousands of years of human interactions, where humans required assistance and experienced face-to-face individual contact to resolve needs, has not abruptly ended. Some worry about global warming, I worry more about interpersonal relationship cooling. I am not a youngster any longer; I am a grown man well into middle to late age. In the past, I would have spent valuable time inflicting negativity on my own soul by trying to persuade others that my journey was the correct path. At this point, I am way past that silliness. Now I understand how individual that pursuit must be. We must remain true to ourselves, and that Higher Power outside ourselves that has always guided our life. If one chooses not to choose a Higher Power, then that in itself is a choice. I do respect that, it's just not my path.

During my interviews, I heard not one uttering of regret, though much of the pain from those years still exist. This team is as incredible today as it was all of those years ago, and confirms my belief that not a one of us showed up in Dover by coincidence. There is another script, playing, with or without, our permission or belief, and each of us is destined to exist within those immutable coordinates. This is not to deny choice. The free will that we each enjoy is a powerful construct, and that power once accepted can change not only your life, but the lives of all those around you. Ultimately, if enough of us accepted this reality, the change would create a better world for us all.

What does it mean to create a better world? It is not an impossible dream. If each person would only work within their own abilities to become the best that they could be, we would see this actuality of a better world. The lesson from our team is that it all starts from within. Regardless of your personal obstacles, if you stay on your true path, you ultimately will succeed. You are bound to stray, that is not a problem. You know what they say, if you're not making mistakes, you're not trying. Very true, but you must correct. Large, incredible changes are not necessary. Each day make a small correction to your path, and ultimately that change will yield huge benefits.

To answer my question of team wellness, I believe yes that we have collectively been able to recover from our shared mortuary experience. After all, what were our options, we have to get better. We are human beings, created by our Maker to assume control over our personal power, and to improve the world. We have now accepted that we are human beings of unlimited power and potential, and it is our personal responsibility to improve our circumstances. Many in this hard and cold world will never make an effort to improve their lives, they will settle for much less than they are capable of. Our team has been offered, and has accepted, an opportunity to intimately understand just how precious and fragile life is. It is a fine line between life and death, and we must try to enjoy this time we have, and to absolutely make the most of that limited time.

Today we are indeed better, and improving incrementally with passing time. There will still be bumps in the road and days where it is not easy to move on our paths. But this is true for all, not just myself, or the DERT Team, or other mortuary workers. Our lives improve with the choices that we make. So we choose, and with support and education those choices will continue to improve. Speaking with old friends from those years has been a complete joy. Hearing their stories, how they remembered the past, then hearing about their current journey. Healing is possible, and if we are able to reach out for help, then improved mental, emotional, and physical health becomes probable.

Writing this during the Florida spring I am very hopeful. Outside the weather is very nearly perfect; with warm days and low humidity to enjoy. I understand that it is my responsibility to care for myself, and purposefully attract others who pursue the same well-being. *If they aren't moving on my path, I will let them be.* I accept this responsibility with all the energy of a living and breathing human being. I know by the Grace of God I have an opportunity to improve my life, as well as the lives of others around me. My time on the mortuary team was a difficult part of my journey in this world, but it was a critical and growth-filled time. It was a time for me that was meant to be, as well as for my team, and now it is time for us to move on.

EPILOGUE

Most mornings I wake up and I feel normal; fully functional, and prepared to positively engage in my schedule for the day. That is the rule, rather than the exception, and I feel extremely thankful to be a productive member of society. I'm working full-time as a human services supervisor with a wonderful group, for an organization that provides important community service. Just like in the military, my first early morning duty is preparing coffee, and then settling in for a day of talking to and serving others. Though I still have difficult moments and days, I have found it extremely helpful to be around supportive and empathetic people. I'm easily restless, and often find the need to get back outside and into the fresh air, if only to recharge.

Four walls remain a challenge, and working in an office is difficult, if I'm not actively engaging my mind. I must make a conscious effort to remain on task, or my thoughts will quickly wander. I'm always most uncomfortable sitting in a group in an enclosed space. If I must be there, the door must be accessible quickly, with me facing a nearby exit. While most areas of my life, as well as my emotional stability have vastly improved since those Dover days, this is one area that seems to have never changed. When placed into the situation of sitting in a small space, I can barely sit still, and there's very little chance I can focus on the issues. I am often anxious during these times, and continue to suffer moments of impatience. Being unable to concentrate in these small meetings is frustrating, and there's no way to explain to others how it feels. So I quietly sit as best I can, and then depart at the first opportunity. Thank goodness for my notes, and the follow-up meeting minutes.

My wife of thirty-one years has always been unconditionally supportive. My son has now returned to live near us in Florida with his fiancé. Life is good now. In the past, I was always careful in my attempts to shield her and my son from the daily traumas faced in the mortuary. It would not have been fair, and trying to explain the pain of that service would be like trying to explain the color of the sky, to a person born blind. There is no way they could have understood how I felt, or how difficult some days still are. I know they've had difficult times understanding some of my actions, and I've sometimes had a difficult time trying to explain my emotions. This being said, it should be noted that their lives had to be influenced by the deep pain in mine. For this I am very sorry to have caused them misery, but I am thankful that they seem to have adjusted so well, and my belief is that the entire family will emerge from the other end of this trauma not only intact, but stronger. Their love has never faltered. I know they love me, and that is supportive enough.

One major lesson I'll take with me from this experience, and the interviews with those who served alongside me, is that we all generally suffer the same long-term recollections, concerns, and fears. Other mortuary members from my team have distinct and similar memories. Some have a history of nightmares, and some do not. We remember the fallen heroes; him or her, and very specific remembrances.

It's not always the matted, bloodied hair, or mangled limbs. Sometimes we remember the blue eyes, or the calm demeanor of their face. As if those dead had accepted their lot. While there's no question many of the death masks were chilled with fright, some did show the warmth of a life well-lived. It feels good to write this down, and to say it out loud. Yes, those dead are still with me, and with some of our team. We are not asking them to leave; but we are validating and trying to understand what they have tried to teach us, or may be teaching us still. This is in no way an ongoing horror, but rather an ongoing blessing that each of my peers must learn to recognize, to rationalize, and ultimately to learn to cope with.

My thought has always been that possibly they are still with me as I am their connection to the world. Indeed, as long as there is breath in body, my thoughts will be with the fallen. I understood after my father passed that this is not an unhealthy belief or thought system. After all, why wouldn't we want to always remember those we cared about most and loved the most? The deceased American heroes that I served in that mortuary are human souls that will forever be a part of what I am. Their families are extensions of that love, and just as I'd serve my own family or team, I'd also be willing to serve those traumatized by the loss of their own American hero. I have discovered many opportunities in this capacity, and will quickly respond to requests for any assistance from any military support organization.

If during the daytime I am triggered to traumatic thoughts, and do begin to regress and think back about those days, I can usually redirect myself back to the moment. Aside from maintaining an active and busy schedule I can step outside for a walk. Near my office is a large, beautiful park surrounding a lake. The lake and circling trail are full of wildlife; alligators, large predatory birds, and turtles. This I enjoy much. Outside enjoying nature allows me some big breaths of deep Florida sunshine, thus placing the entire situation into perspective. Being out there always reminds me of the old Jimmy Buffett song, *"Breathe in, breathe out, move on."* This is such a simple idea, but it works nearly every time. If that does not work, then I will make a call to family or friends. The fact is that life is good and getting better. I am physically safe, and will not be placed back into the mortuary. These realizations alone most always guide me back to my positive thoughts. I am fortunate to have friends and family that care about me, and would be willing to do anything to help. I am indeed a very lucky man.

Even more fortunately for me, today the nightmares are extremely rare. I suppose if I would have a nightmare and wake up at 5 AM it would be more tolerable, but generally if I have one I'm cold-sweating and awake at 1 AM. When dreaming about the mortuary, my mind is actually back in those years. These nights turn into very long next days. It is amazing what the unconscious mind is able to remember. Today the dreams are much less distinct with more variation. Though the theme remains the same, the trauma seems to be easing. Many of those faces and events may never leave me, and I am not trying to chase them away. It is because of that experience that I am exactly where I am supposed to be today. It is as everything that has happened since does not exist. The mind is incredible, horrible and beautiful at the exact same time. Today, I am grateful for my life and my family, and I am extra grateful that those dreams today are very, very rare.

I do have a Veteran's Administration eligibility card, but to be honest I have not been consistent in regularly attending my appointments. I do enjoy visiting the facility, and speaking to staff, sitting in the waiting room and chatting. I'd like to go talk to a counselor about my thoughts and my memories, but I just don't believe it would help. I am fully rational and understand that's a lousy excuse and my own fault for not trying, but I believe what I believe. I feel that I have progressed in my recovery very well, and will maintain my personal path. If I ever do need help, I know who to contact. What I have found to help me most today is the same thing that helped me most back when I served on active duty and was working in the mortuary. That is service to others, the kindness of others, and being able to talk and share as friends. I never talk details about the horror that was our duty in the mortuary, but most of my friends and peers know I was in military service, and some even know I worked among the dead.

On the other hand, I always keep my civilian medical appointments for physical ailments, and take my medicine as directed. I have never told my primary care doctor about the occasional nightmares. It isn't that I couldn't tell her, but the story is just too long, and ultimately, who would it help? I am not going to take any medications for anxiety or depression. That is out of the question. Besides, I know how to solve each of those ailments. It's called getting off my lazy behind. Don't get me wrong, I understand depression and anxiety may be a chemical imbalance for some, but for me personally I am convinced that it is situational. I will share that *if you are one of those old veterans* suffering depression and still using alcohol, please rethink your actions. I promise you are on the wrong path. Alcohol remains depressant number one, and a potent enemy to those trying to recover from a depressed state. If you are addicted, seek help. At this point, I feel fortunate to be independent, gainfully employed and reasonably healthy. A little more exercise and better diet would certainly be helpful.

Old friends are missed, especially those that served with me in Dover all those years ago. They are quick to understand how I feel, and I wouldn't hesitate to share with them any thoughts or concerns I have had past or present. Living just south of Orlando has taken me away from most of those mortuary teammates, so working on this project ultimately turned into an effective therapeutic exercise, as well as a chance to catch up with those old friends. Being able to speak to them via phone was at times emotionally difficult, often revealing in the way I've thought about the emotional trauma of those years. Ultimately, and above all, those phone calls were healing. I've learned that many of my remembrances and feelings from those days gone by are shared feelings. It's good to know I'm not alone, nor ever will be.

I paraphrased the team's thoughts and words when I could, and always respected their wishes to be named, or remain private. I tried not to inject my own meanings into what the team shared. However that was very difficult. Blending the memory of the past from different points of view is always bound to create results somewhere based in the middle of each of our truths. My goal from the beginning of this project was to honestly document the ordeal of the entire team. I've found that difficult to do, as my own perceptions continue to flood into my thoughts and my writing. I realize the casual reader will not perceive the difference, but my team will. I only hope they can forgive me.

Today we live in a strange, almost unrecognizable world from the one that I grew up in. In 1979, I would have never imagined a computer in every home, and how that access to information would change the way we all perceive the world around us. We are voyeurs; able to peer into others' lives, to view other societies, and ways of life in near real-time. Our ability to learn and gain insight into history and science are unparalleled in written human history. Our children are much better educated, and their futures are unlimited. Imagine the child born this year or next. It is likely they will be roaming this earth in the year 2100. At that time, eighty years old may not be end of life. Living to one hundred may be routine. What will that world look like? I remember an analogy made to me once that a child born in the late nineteenth century, with nary an automobile on the road, incredibly was alive to see a human being walk on the moon. My wife recently purchased me a Fitbit Blaze, and I am astonished and amazed at how easily it tracks my physical well-being, including my exercise, resting pulse and sleep habits. Where will human civilization be in another eighty years? Only time will tell the extent of human progress, but one thing for sure is that human beings will continue to challenge all boundaries.

Especially in the United States, each of us regardless of background have opportunity today, and that freedom of thought will ultimately make life better for all of us. You may not believe this by watching the cable news or following social media, but it is true. Our lives for better or worse are the result of the choices that we make and our individual responsibility. America has a history of oppression towards women and minorities, but our nation is leaps and bounds ahead of most of the world. The real problem may very well be how we see and treat ourselves. How do we love ourselves, and those immediately around us? Our culture has turned away from faith, and this decision seems to be haunting us all. Though I am dedicated to keep politics out of this book, the division in our country needs to be addressed. Not just by me in this writing, but by each of us in our daily lives. Each of us has a responsibility to reach out in kindness, and to try to make life a little better for those around us.

My personal obstacles to improving my life have usually been my own actions, and my own temperament. I have made mistakes, and have not always surrounded myself with those determined to live a positive life. Sometimes I have over-reacted to situations, confused and angry, before thinking about the repercussions of those actions. It has taken most of my fifty-some years to accept who and what I am. If you find yourself with a similar struggle, just try to relax, and always remember that you have ultimate responsibility for your destiny. The ultimate outcome of your life will not be decided by your parents, your peers, or some government agency, but rather you alone are ultimately responsible. Once you are able to accept this responsibility, your life will immediately begin to improve. This is a large responsibility, because your decisions will affect many of those closest to you. However, you are capable of accomplishing this reality, and making your life the best it can be.

My life has mostly been one of hope, always surrounded by friends and family that love me, so I have no excuse for any of my poor actions or outcomes. I know that whenever in my life I've worked extra hard, I have enjoyed extra luck. I know that when I have treated others with kindness, then kindness has been returned. Of course there are exceptions, but don't let those few distract you from the beautiful world that you and your family deserve. Life has always been exactly what I have made of it. I suspect the same would work for you, or any of those around you. When you begin to care about and love yourself, you will find another path quickly opening. So it is today, so it has always been. Our reality is defined by us, and no matter the difficulty we face, it's ultimately how we view that reality that decides our future.

So, what has America learned, or declined to learn following the events of 9/11? Why can't our society come together as one, and focus on the similarities and love rather than division and hate? Hate we do, and it's easily viewed daily by all members of our nation, and indeed around the world through the American media. The media gains ratings through conflict, and doesn't seem able to just share the facts. Rather, they are determined to tell us how to feel about it and which side is right. Even more incredible, you can read on the internet or watch on television any information that deepens your convictions. If you want to believe that aliens are observing our planet from the far side of Mars, then you can find an entire group of people who believe the exact same thing. Educate yourself, and always openly consider and question your beliefs. Do not let others influence your free will. Individual and original thought remain rare. Each of us is compelled and free to choose. While free choice and free will are incredible benefits of life in America, there are consequences of our choices. Our nation seems to have lost its moral compass, and many in America are suffering. America is indeed divided, but it is not too late. America is a chosen nation, and will recover. This I will always believe.

Over fifteen years have passed, but in many ways time has stood still. Dover's *legacy for service continues today.* Since September 11th, 2001 the mortuary team has helped identify and return home American heroes from Iraq and Afghanistan who have paid the ultimate price for our freedom. Mortuary staff members have continued to rotate and change in the face of PCS and retirements. However, one thing remains the same today, as it was yesterday and will be tomorrow. The Dover port mortuary staff serves with honor and distinction and continues to embody the Air Force ideals of integrity first, service before self, and excellence in all we do. Let me assure all who read this that serving with this mortuary team at Dover was the highlight of my seven assignments, 21-year, and 18-day active-duty military career.

Though I did not expect to be healed on this writing journey, I did hope to gain increased insight into why I continue to struggle from that trauma of all those years ago. Even more, I hoped to find the path forward. Knowing first hand that my journey was the team's journey has allowed me to accept the reality of my feelings and my present circumstance. I believe in this sense, that completion of this journey was accomplished. Along with insight I have gained even more hope, and more motivation to move forward. The DERT Team of Dover were an incredible group of young Americans, destined to serve their country honorably in that mortuary, and it was a high honor to be among them. I loved them then, and still do today. I only hope that I've honored their legacy with this manuscript, and I hope that it helps each of us to heal just a bit more, and to move a little further, quietly along life's long and unpredictable highway. Above all, I hope and pray that our service is never forgotten.

Our team *was only a very small part* of the overall Dover mortuary mission. Our team universally responded gratefully and effectively as a small part of that larger mission. Our team was very proud to share that mission, and assist in returning our fallen heroes home. Today more than ever I fully believe that God brought us together to achieve what none of us could have accomplished alone. Not one member has ever been more, or less valuable, than any other. Every single member has made me proud to be a part of something greater than myself, and a part of something that will stand long after we are all gone.

My hope is that if you have taken the time to purchase, invest your time, and read this book that you come away with a greater perspective of what life was like for those serving during those years. If you have enjoyed it, and find yourself with a greater appreciation for our service members, I hope that you will share that appreciation at every opportunity. For my peers in military service, especially those that served alongside me during those years, this book is dedicated to you. If it is one of my old DERT Team members reading this very sentence, and you are wondering, "Does he mean me?" Yes, it is for you. It is documentation of our sacrifice and love for one another, for our fallen heroes, and for this great nation. At the moment where your fellow citizens needed you most, you stepped up and made us all proud.

The moment that those planes slammed into the World Trade Center many American lives were changed forever. It hasn't been easy, but I would not change any one of the moments that followed. God always provides a way to accomplish what does not seem possible. There's no doubt His hand guided this team through those tragic and unpredictable early days, and in fact He remains a distinct presence in those still serving in that hallowed building. Some reading this may or may not believe it, and though I didn't always exude faith, I've always known the truth. God Bless every single service-member; past, present, and future, and God Bless America.